AF263700

ONE FOGGY MORNING IN SUMMER

In the Creasey Mahan Nature Preserve

ALSO EXPLORE THESE BOOKS IN THE CREASEY MAHAN COLLECTION

One Foggy Morning in Winter
One Foggy Spring Morning
Spring
Summer

ONE FOGGY MORNING IN SUMMER

In the Creasey Mahan Nature Preserve

Photography by Karin Acree

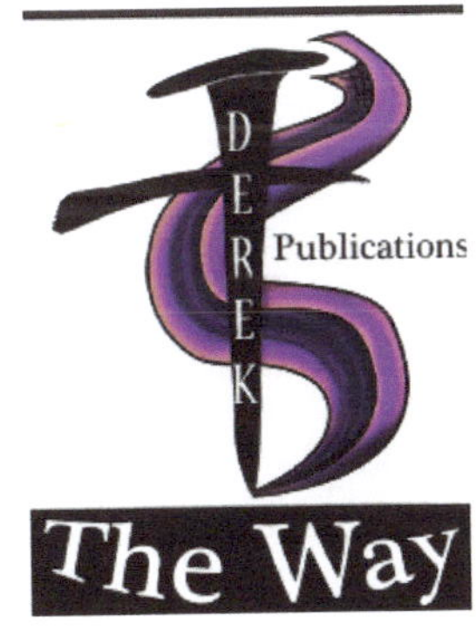

DEDICATION

To my friends
Michele
and
Brittany

FORWARD
About the Creasey Mahan Collection

Karin's books represent well the words of poet and philosopher, Henry David Thoreau: "Heaven is under our feet as well as over our heads." Each photograph in this series captures a cherished moment – raindrops that look like jewels, a lightning bug as it rests on a leaf, sunlight streaming through trees and a Red-tailed Hawk soaring overhead. Her images are like prayers that remind us to slow down, enjoy each moment and behold every blessing that may appear before us.

When Karin first showed me her photographs and the accompanying passages contained in this series of scripture books, I was in awe of her talent, dedication and the many hours she spent alone and with her daughters, as they walked the scenic trails at Creasey Mahan Nature Preserve. The quotes that accompany the photographs match each image perfectly.

My hope is that you, the reader, will take time to let each image and scripture wash over you. Karin's books invite us to walk alongside her as she notices that "He has made everything beautiful in its time." (Ecclesiastes 3:11)

continued...

Creasey Mahan Nature Preserve is a public charity that serves nearly 50,000 visitors each year. Visitors may enjoy 170-acres of rolling hills, open grasslands, year-round streams, nine-miles of trails and a two-acre woodland garden. Families appreciate the annual events, Thrive Forest School programs, Forest Friends Playground and the Nature Center. Creasey Mahan is open 365 days a year from dawn to dusk.

By Tavia Cathcart Brown
Executive Director of Creasey Mahan Nature Preserve

Yours is the day, yours also the night;
you have established the heavenly lights and the sun.
PSALM 74:16 (ESV)

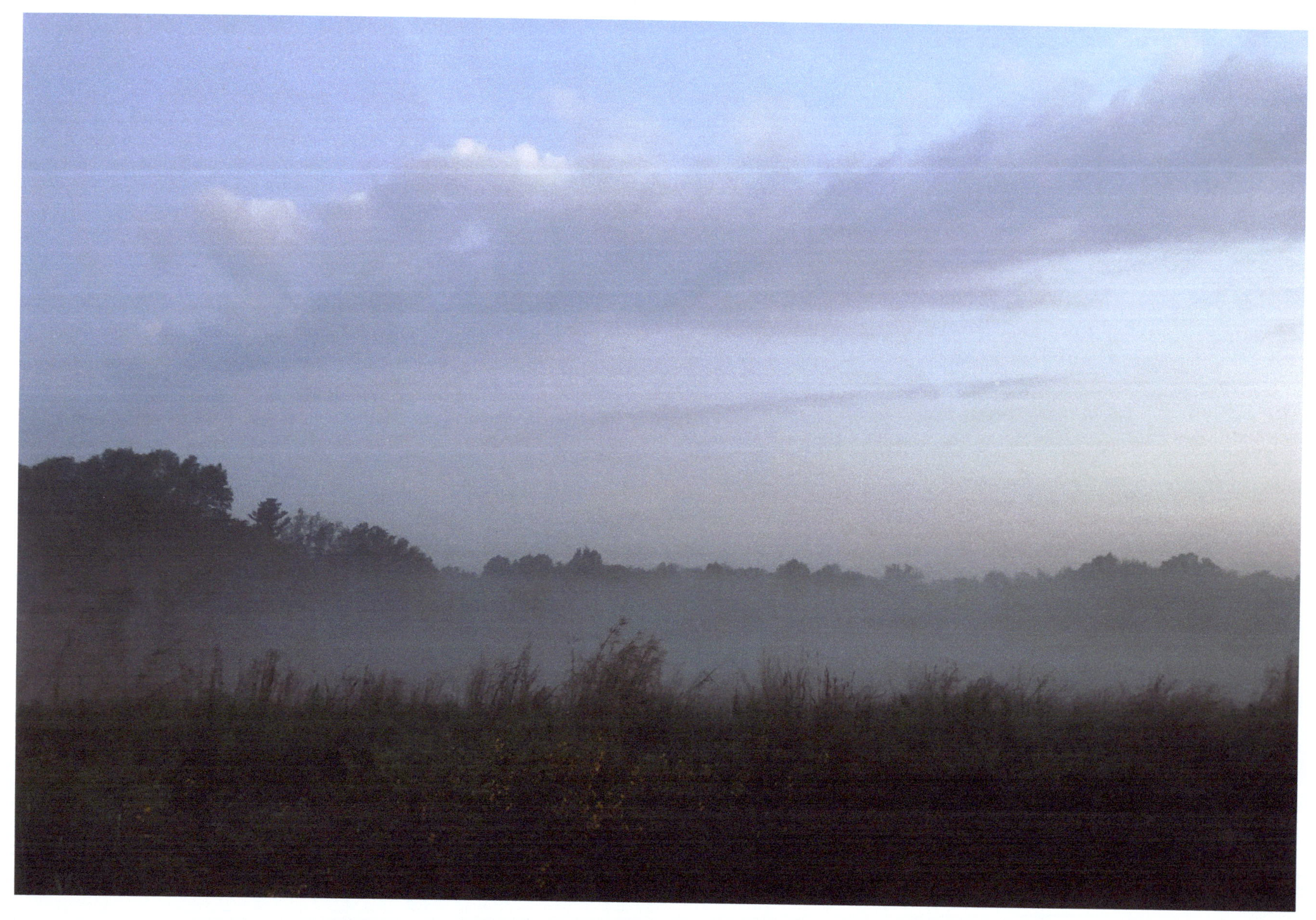

Arise, walk about the land through its length and breadth;
for I will give it to you.
GENESIS 13:17-18 (NASB)

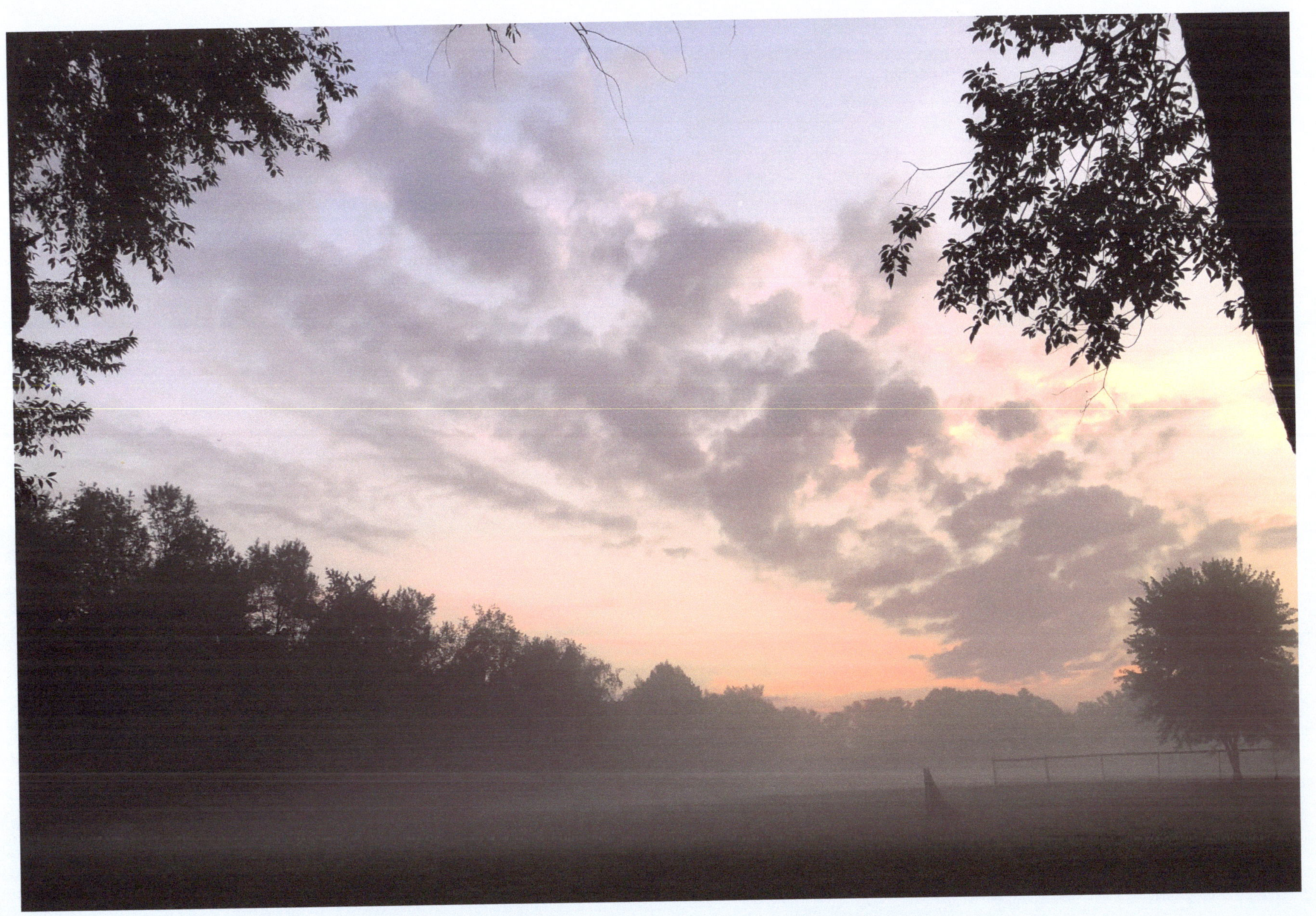

The heavens are telling of the glory of God;
And the expanse is declaring the work of His hands.
PSALM 19:1 (NASB)

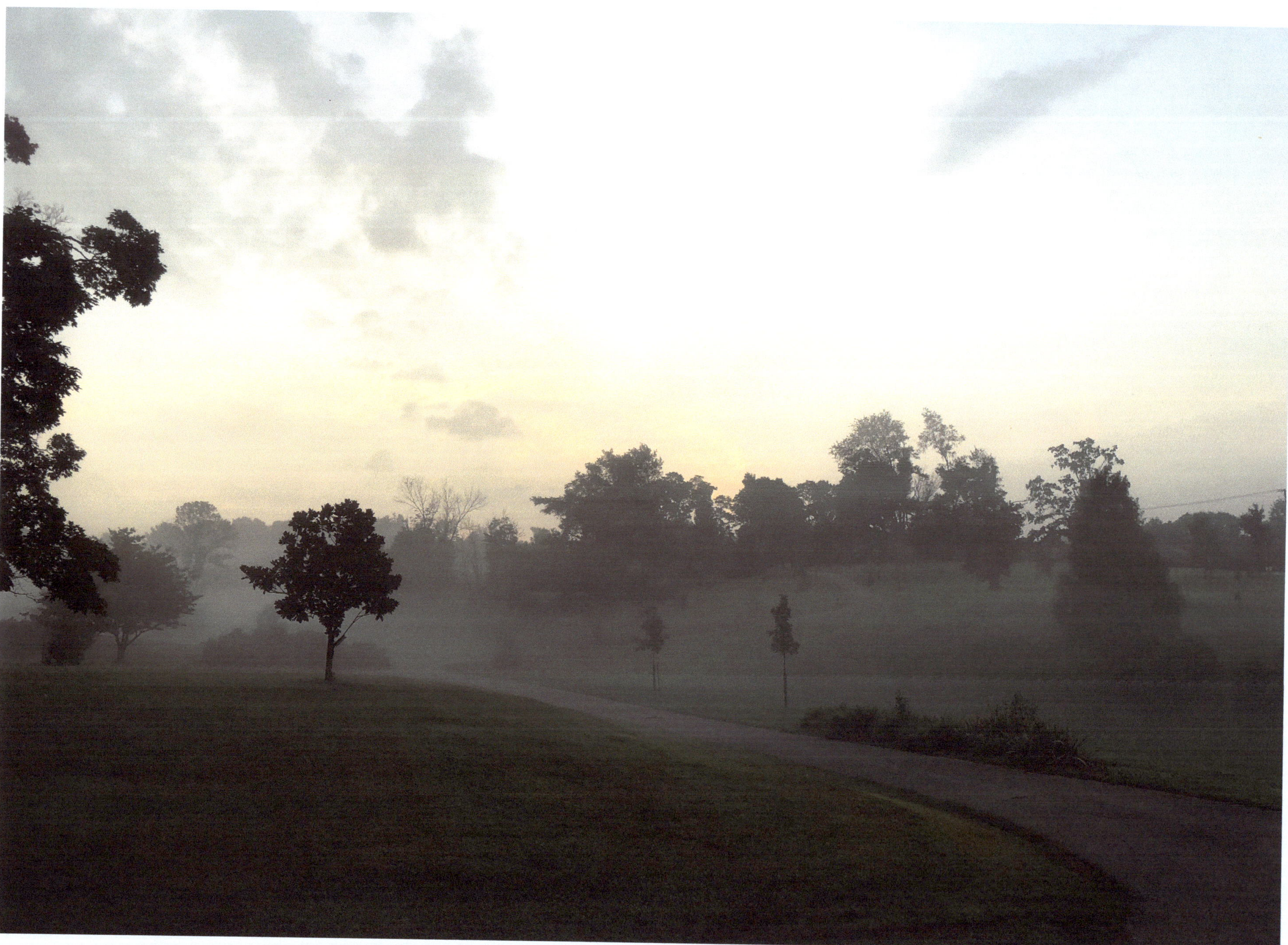

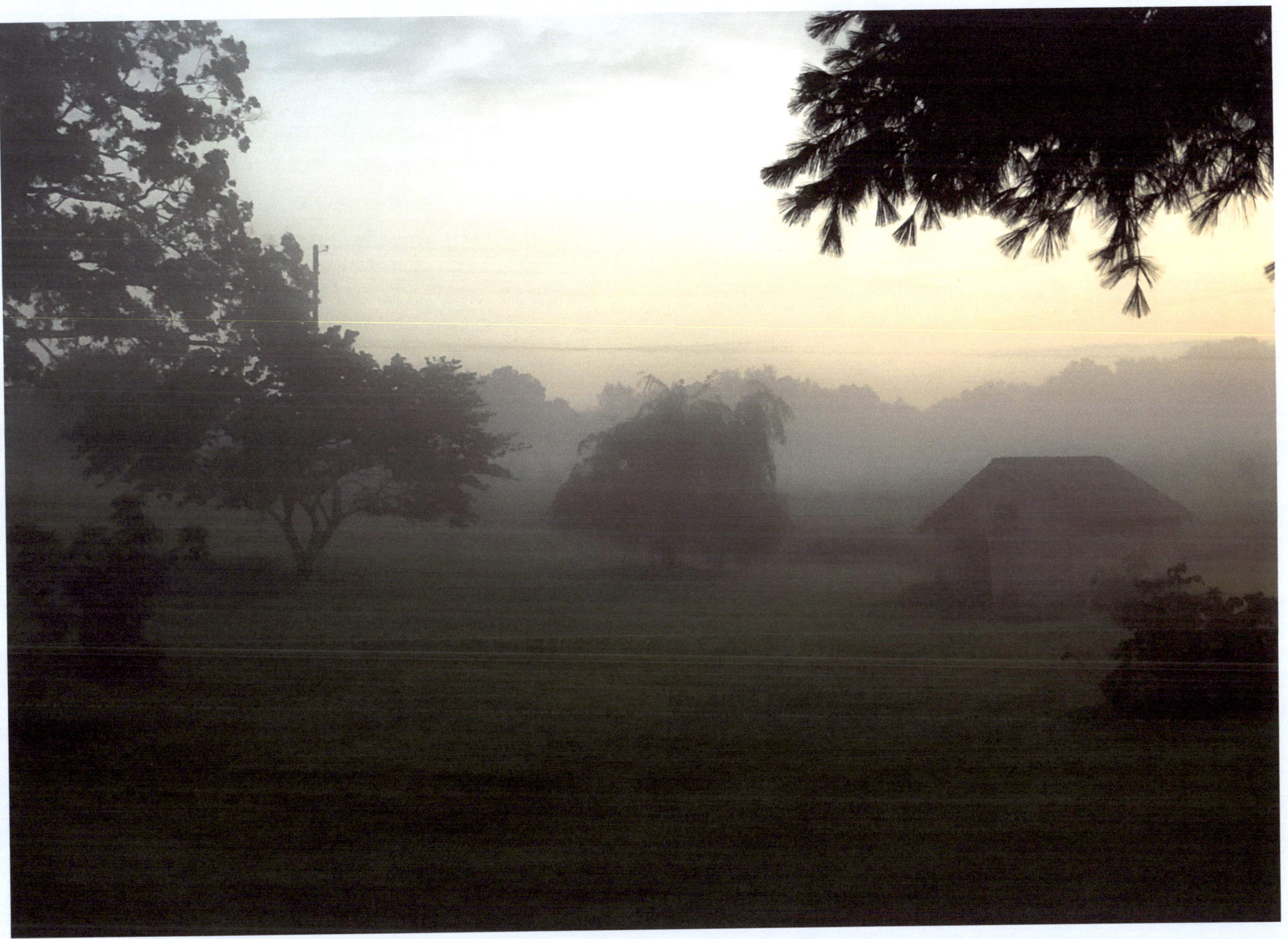

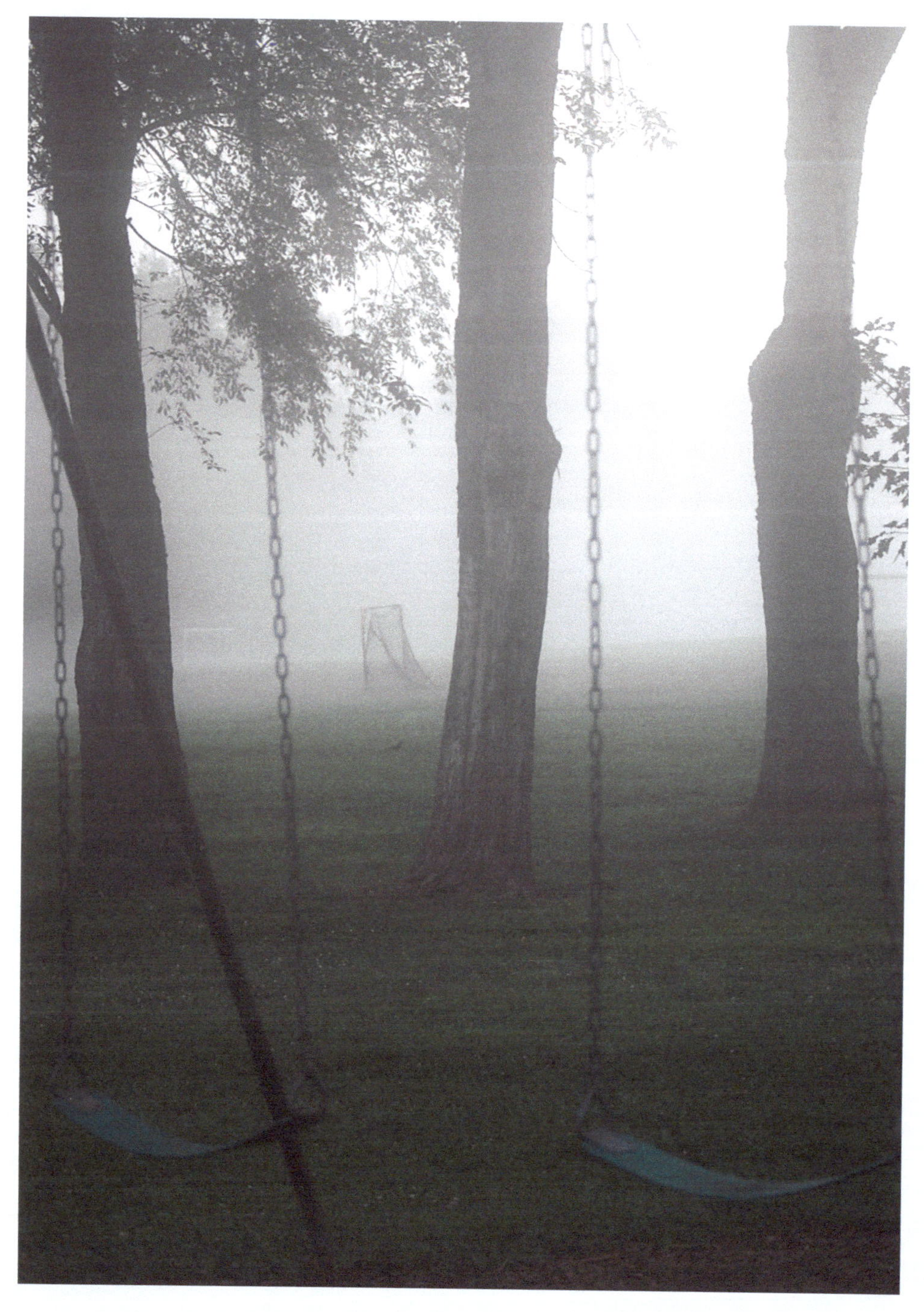

I have told you all this so that you may have
peace in me.
Here on earth you will have many trials
and sorrows. But take heart,
because I have overcome the world.
JOHN 16:33 (NLT)

*Every good thing given
and every perfect gift is from above,
coming down from the Father of lights,
with whom there is no variation
or shifting shadow.*
JAMES 1:17 (NASB)

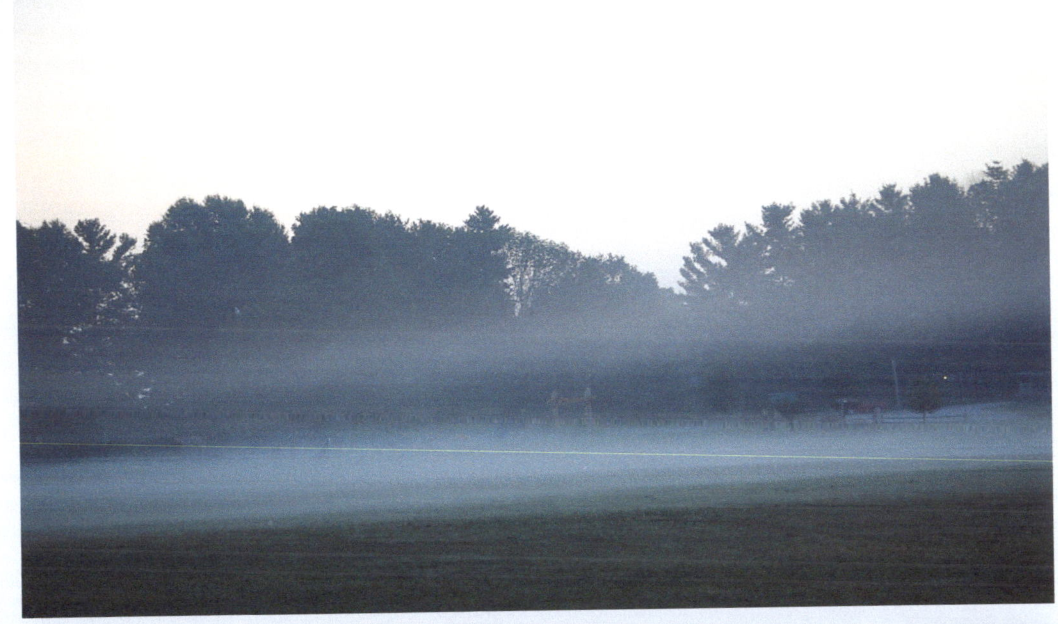

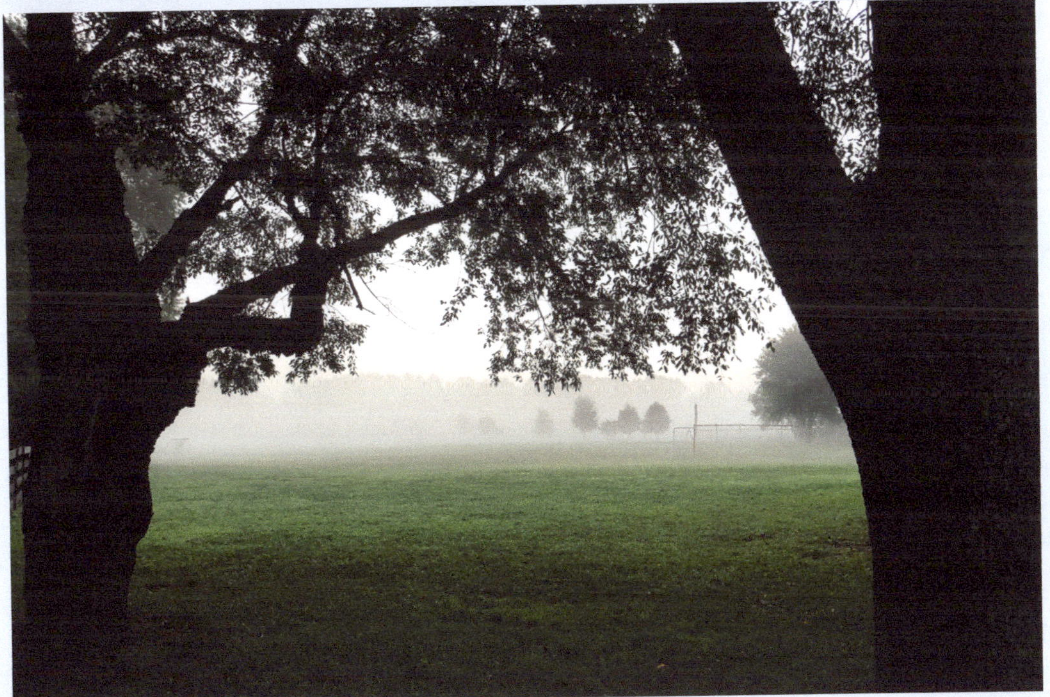

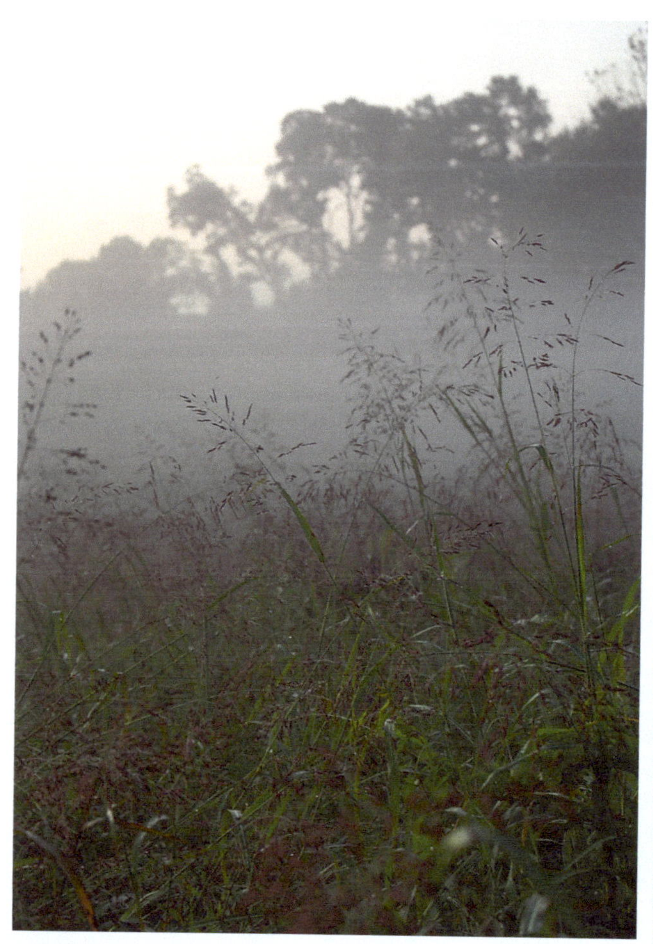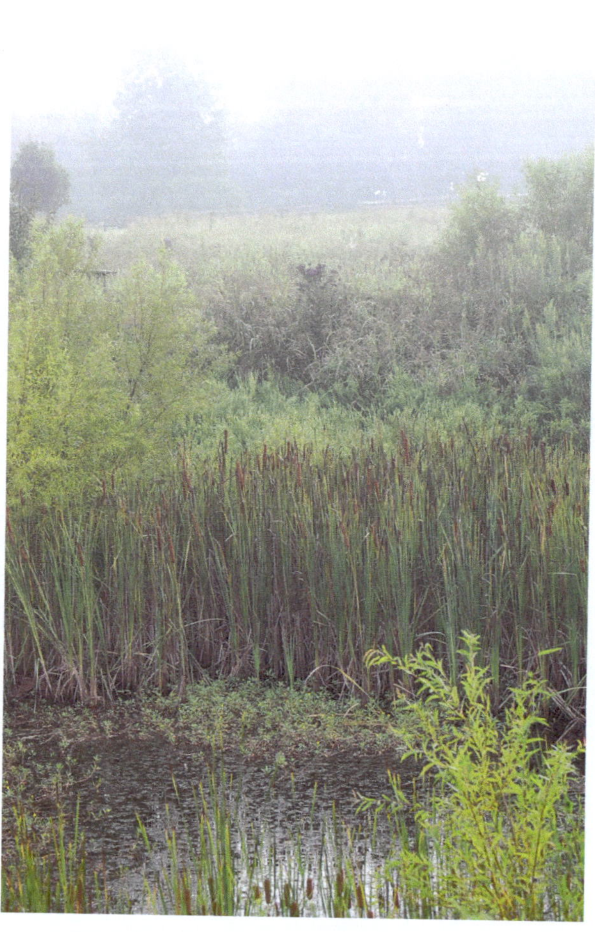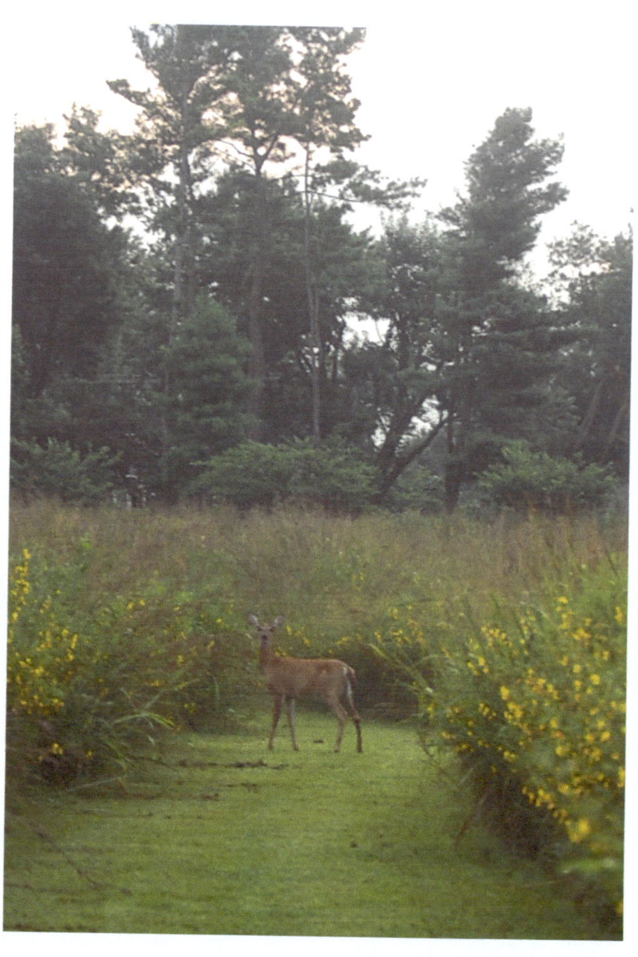

The Kingdom of Heaven is like a treasure that a man discovered hidden in a field.

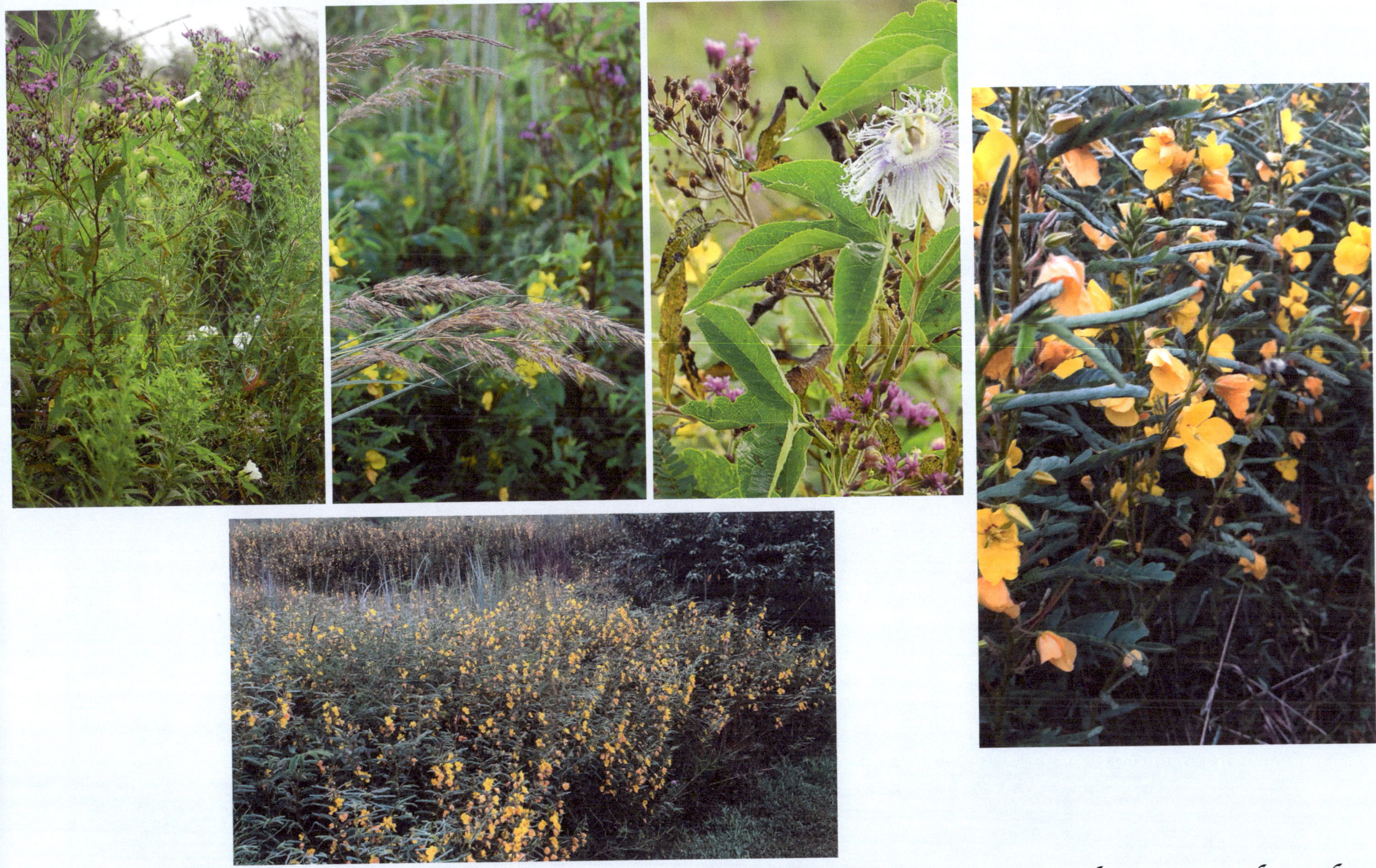

In his excitement, he hid it again and sold everything he owned to get enough money to buy the field. - MATTHEW 13:44 (NLT)

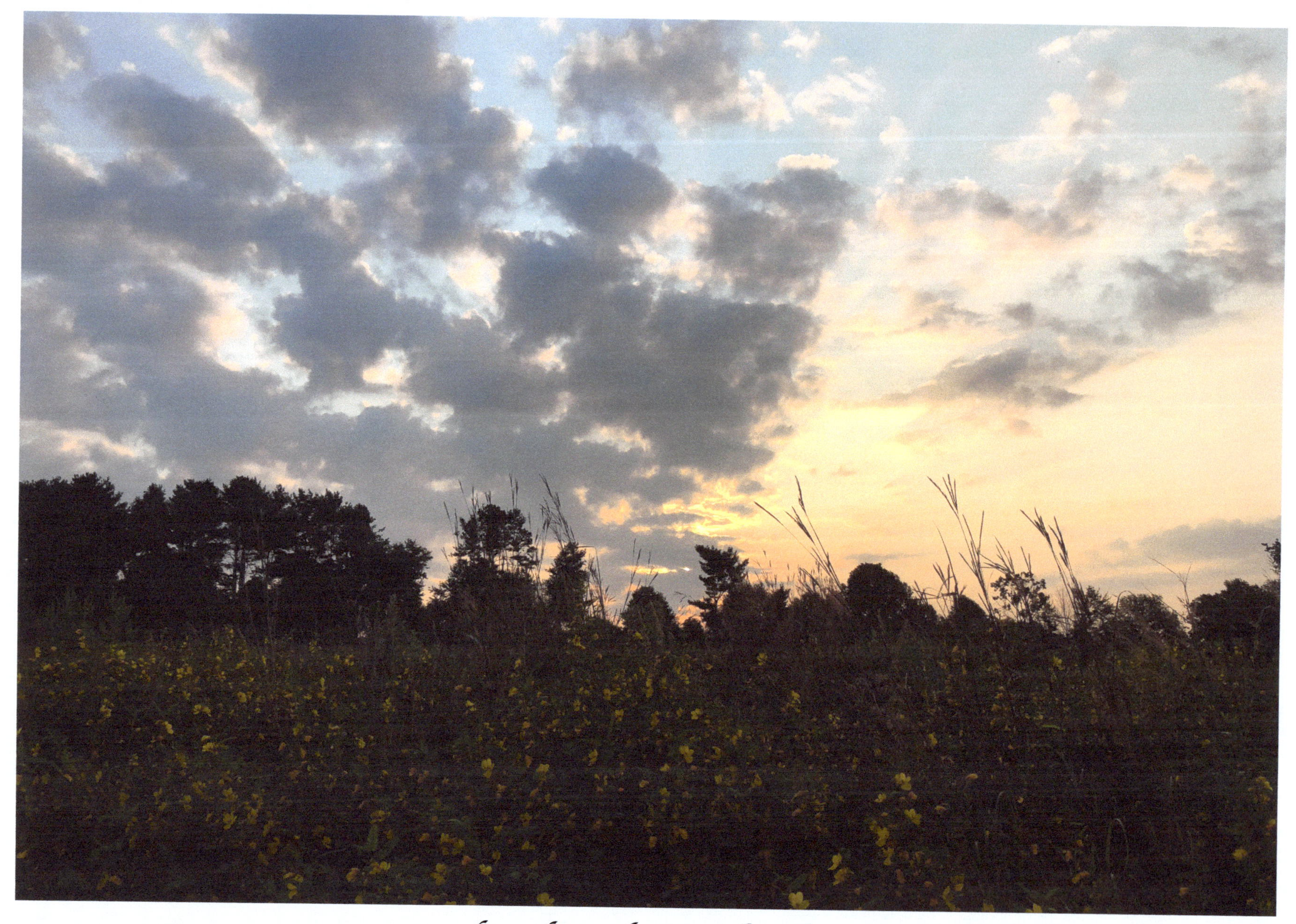

but they who wait for the LORD shall renew their strength;

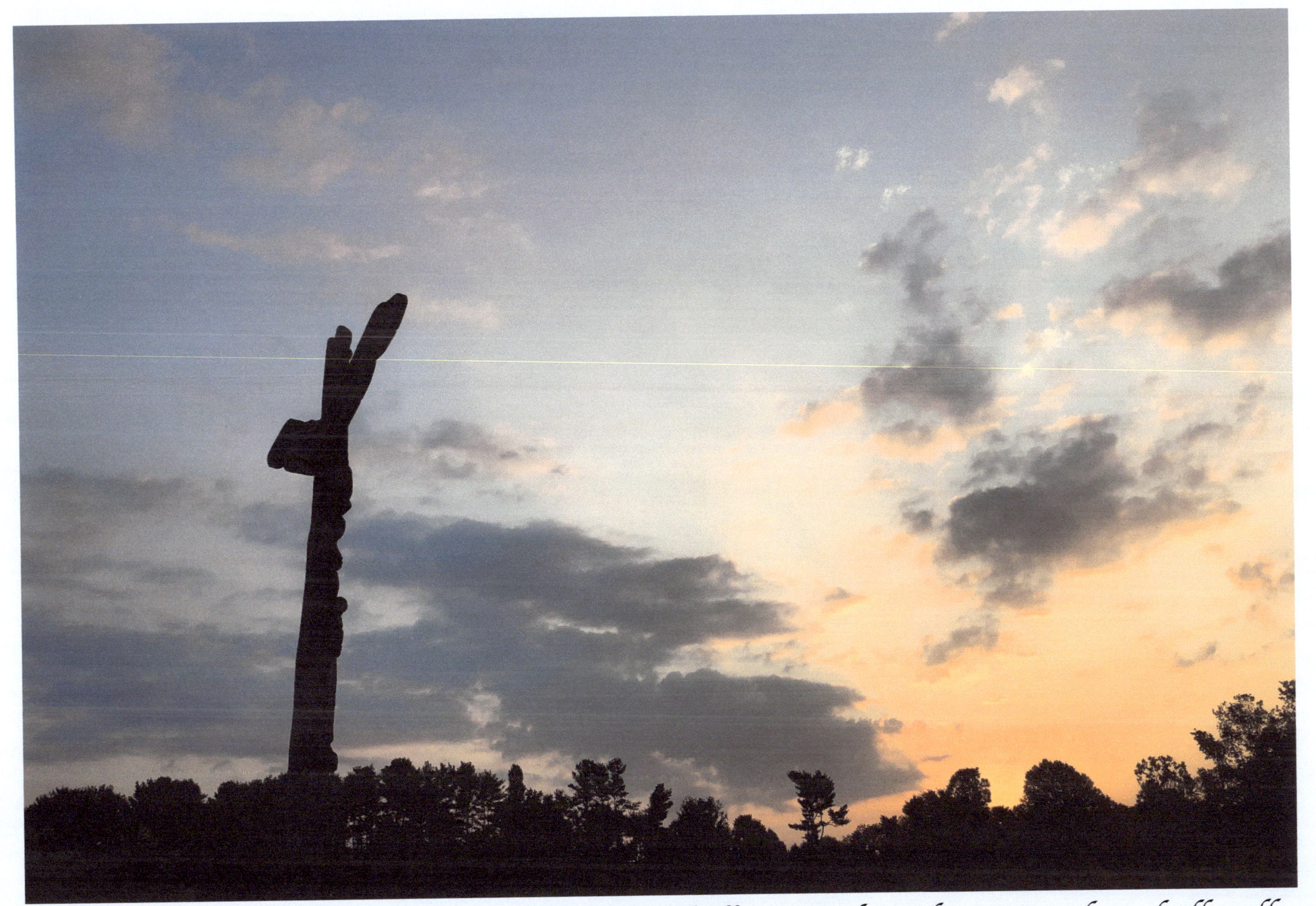

they shall mount up with wings like eagles; they shall run and not be weary; they shall walk and not be faint. - ISAIAH 40:31 (ESV)

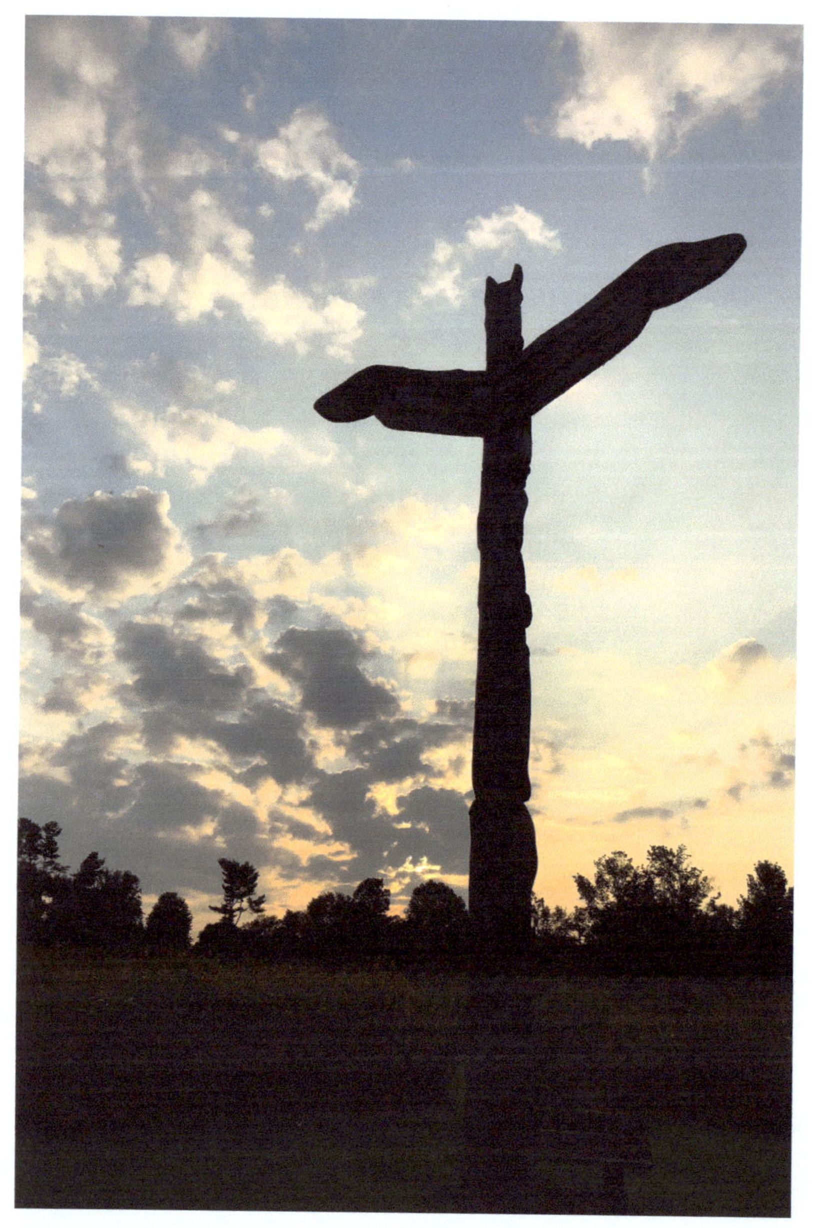

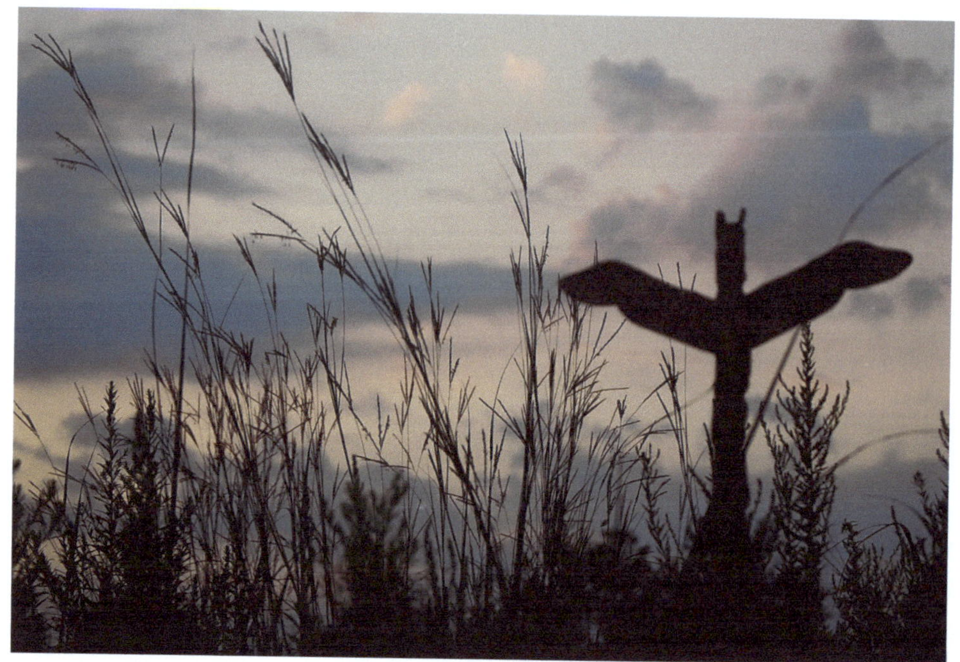

Praise the LORD, my soul,
and forget not all his benefits -
who forgives all your sins and heals all your diseases,
who redeems your life from the pit
and crowns you with love and compassion,
who satisfies your desires with good things
so that your youth is renewed like the eagle's.
PSALM 103:2-5 (NIV)

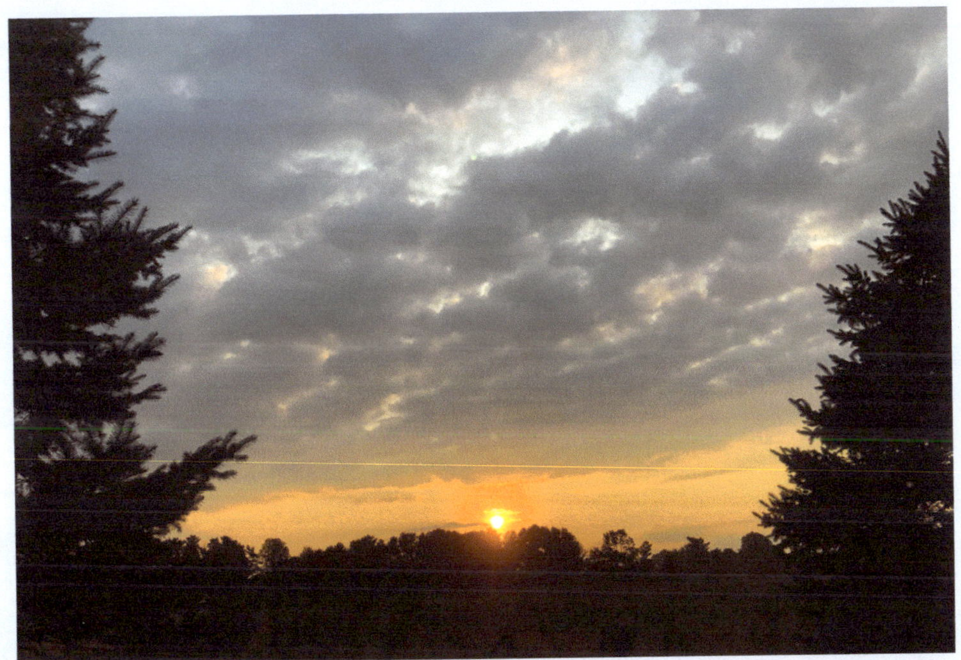

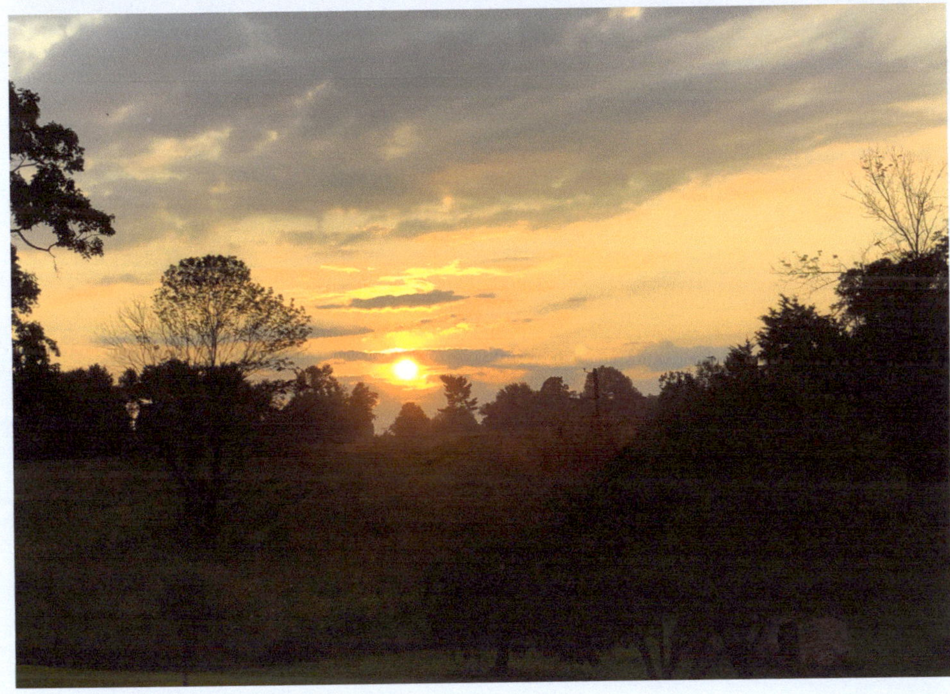

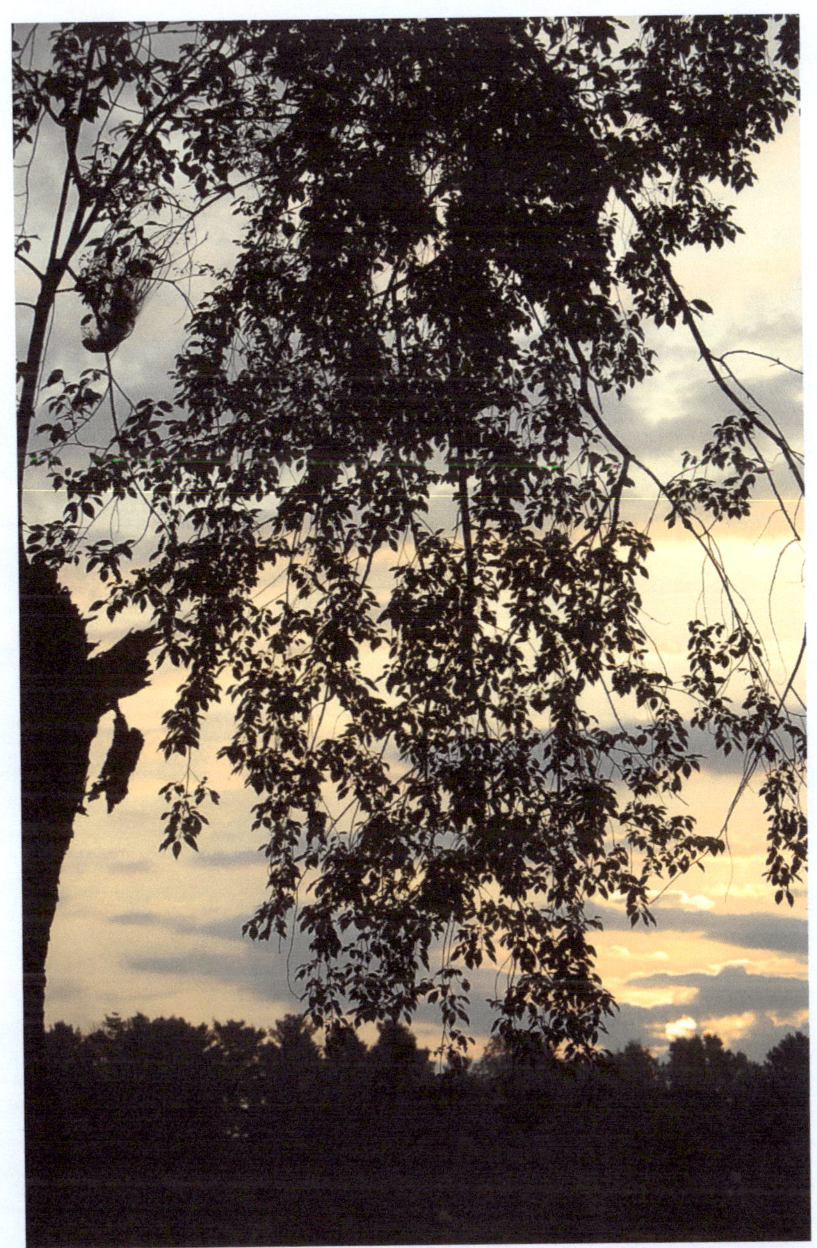

Because of God's tender mercy, the morning light from heaven is about to break upon us
LUKE 1:78 (NLT)

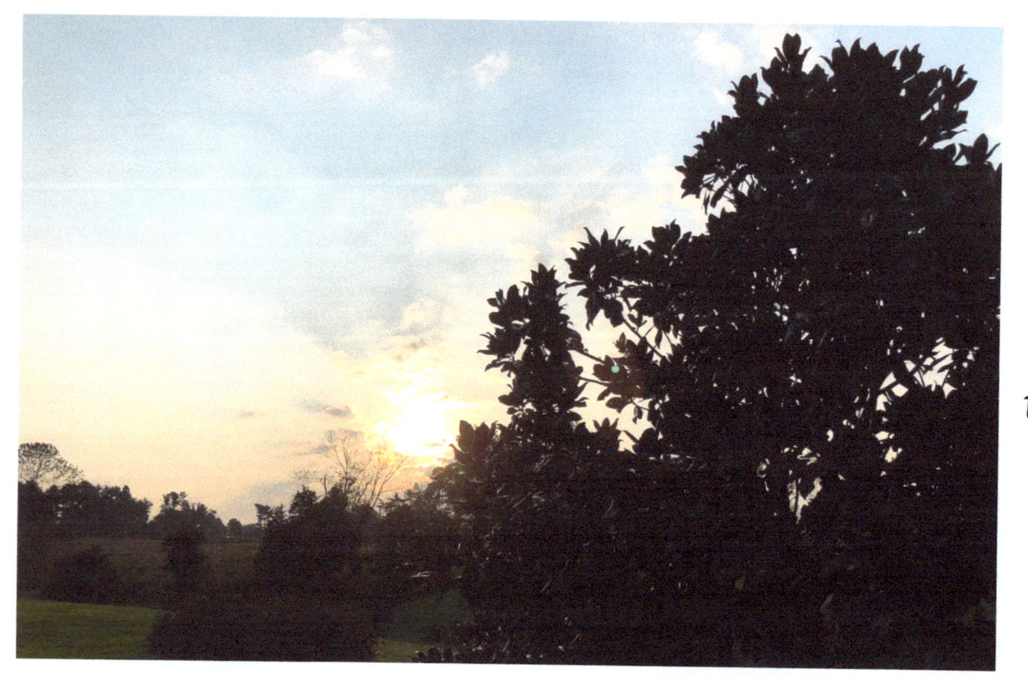

Have you commanded the morning
since your days began,
and caused the dawn to know its place,
that it might take hold of the skirts of the
earth... - JOB 38:12-13 (ESV)

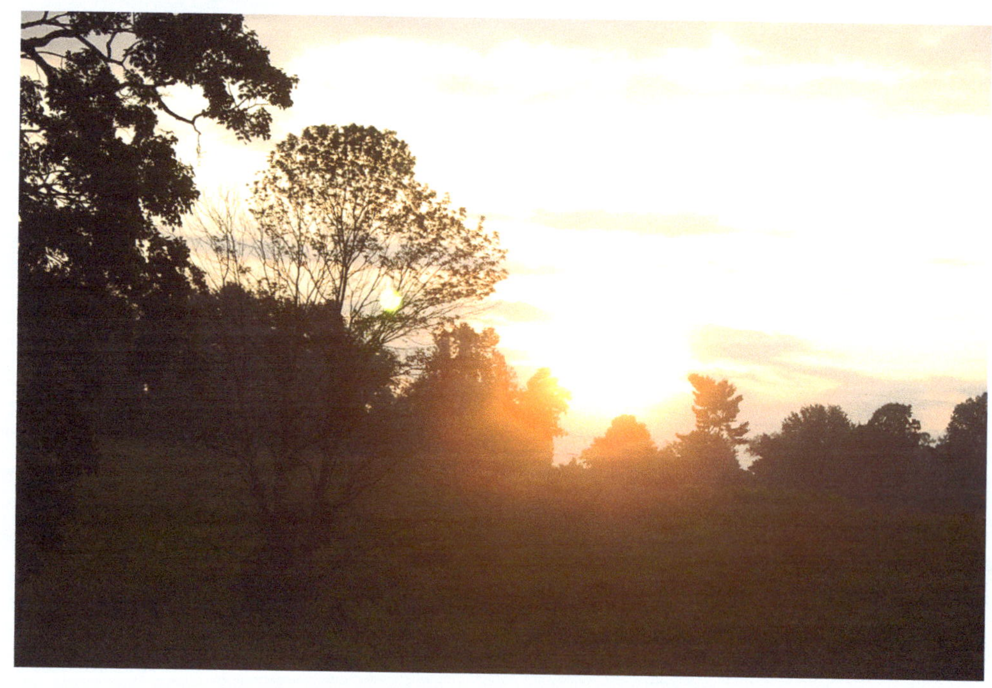

Then your light shall break forth like the morning,

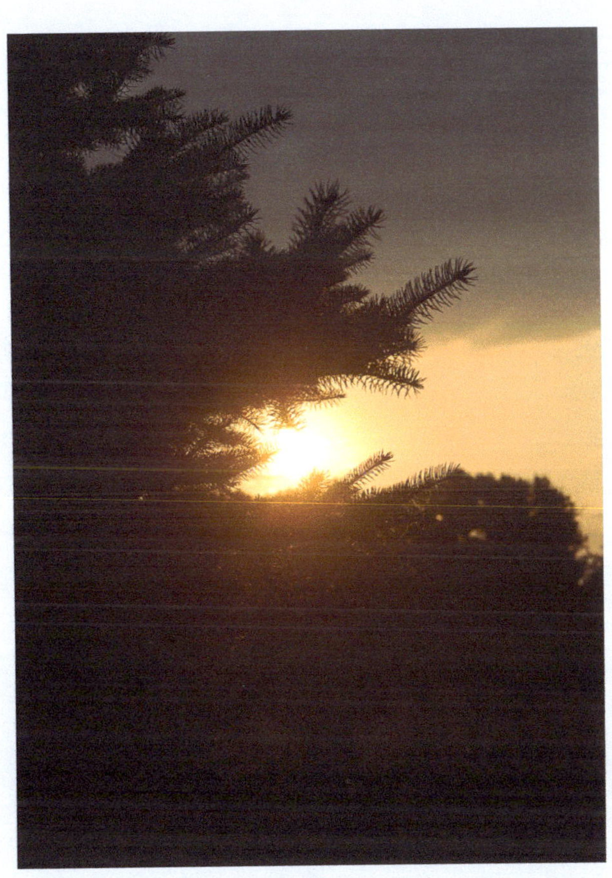

Your healing shall spring forth speedily,
And your righteousness shall go before you;
The glory of the LORD shall be your rear guard.
ISAIAH 58:8 (NKJV)

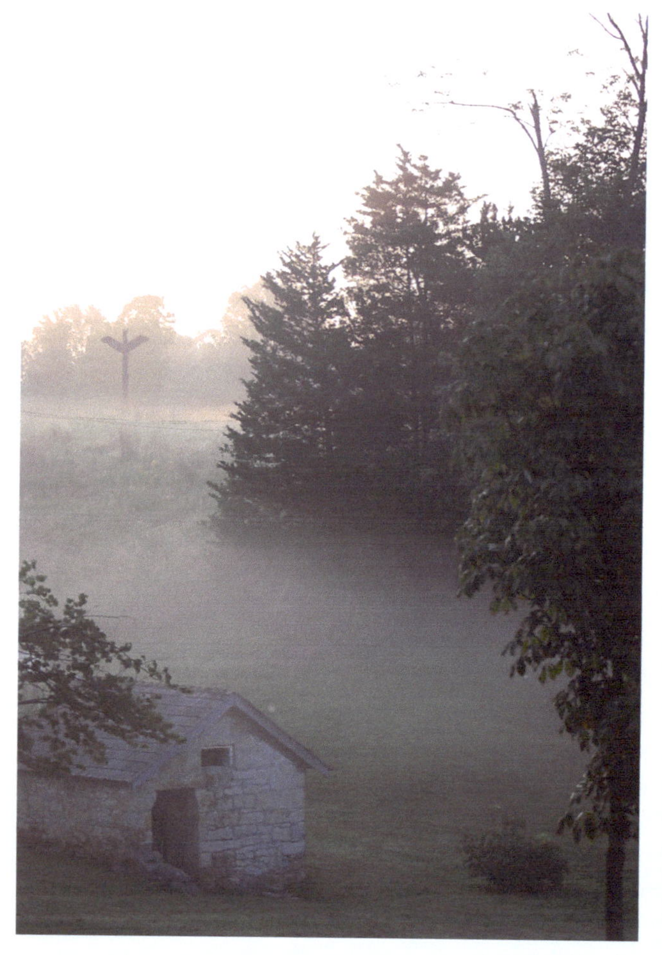 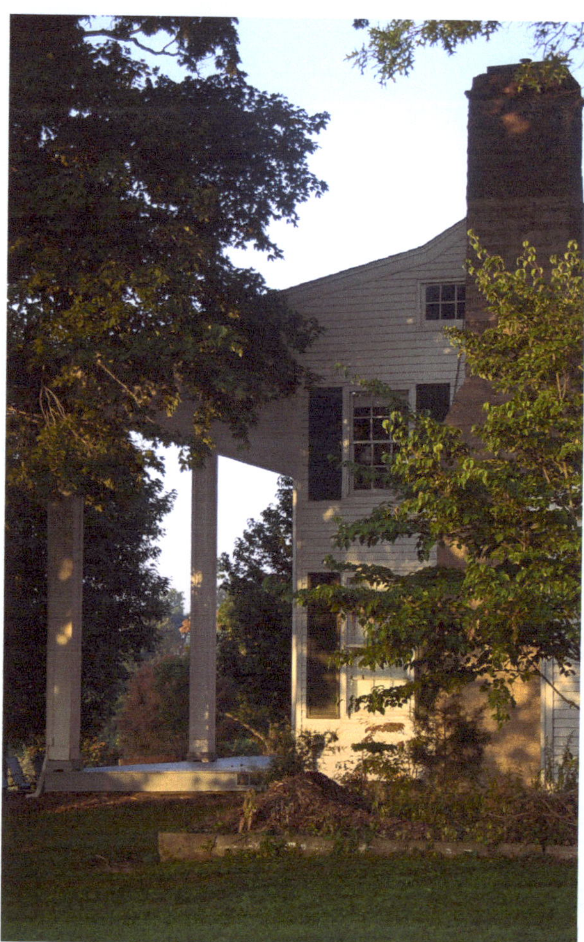 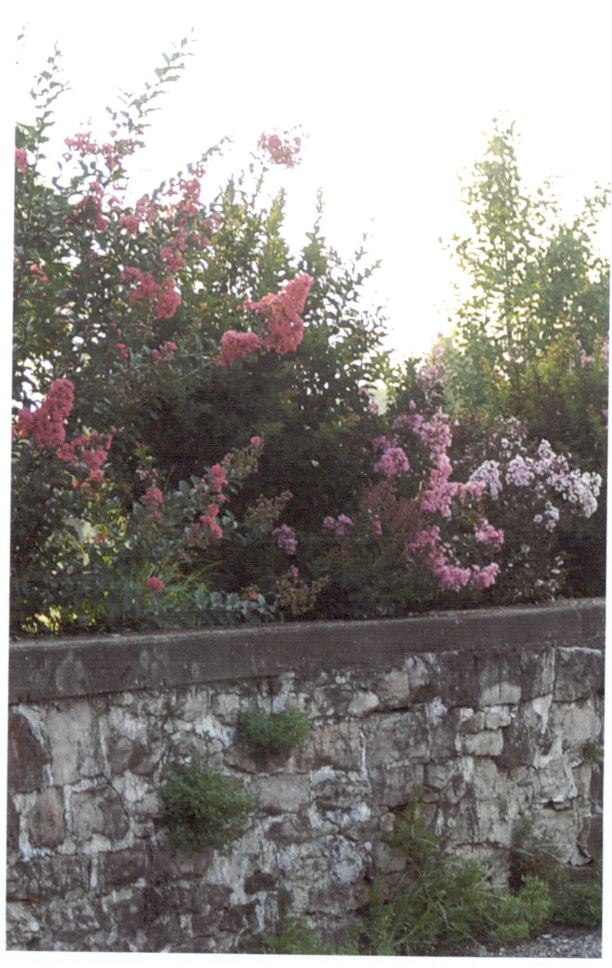

Don't let your hearts be troubled.
Trust in God, and trust also in me.
There is more than enough room in my Father's home.
JOHN 14:1-2 (NLT)

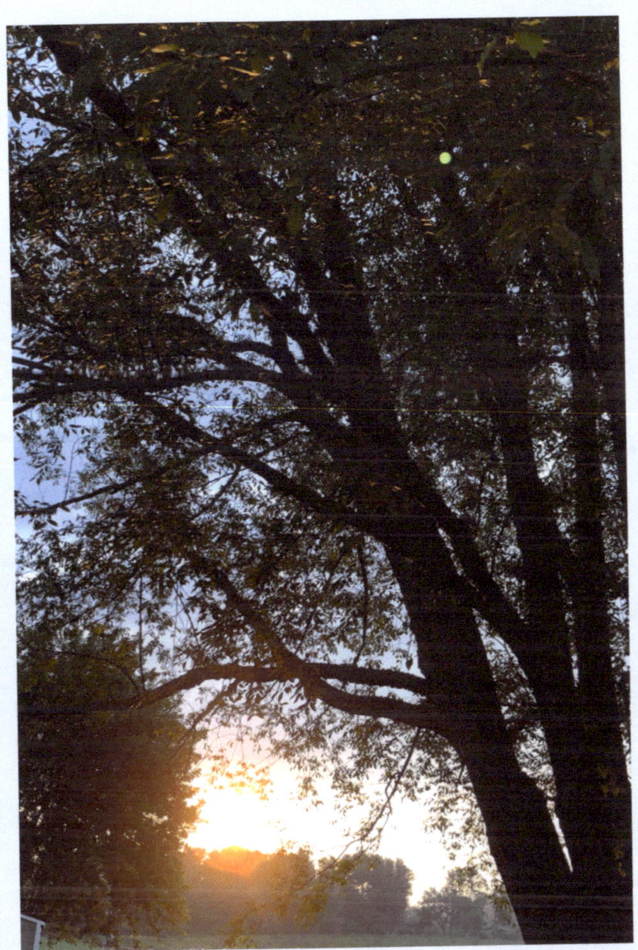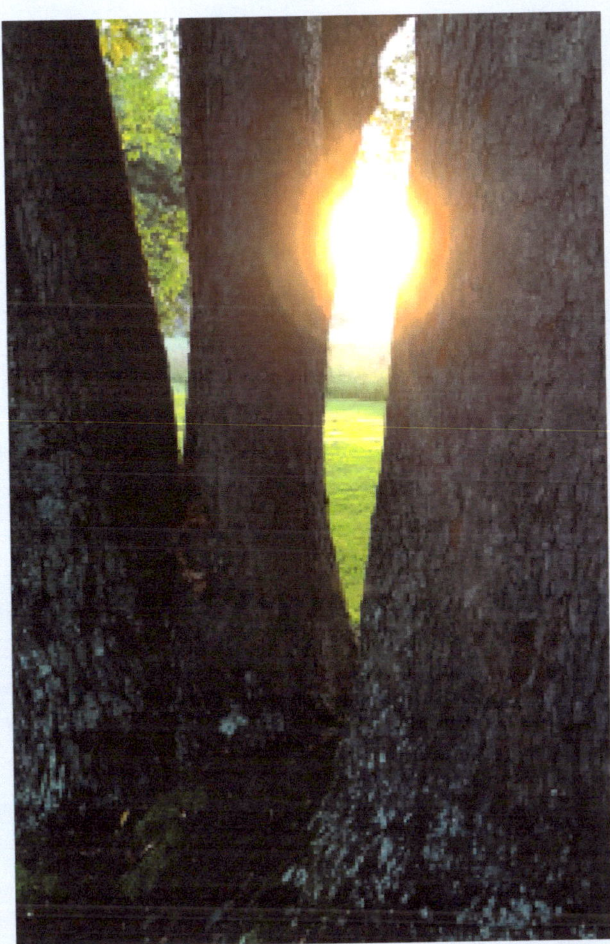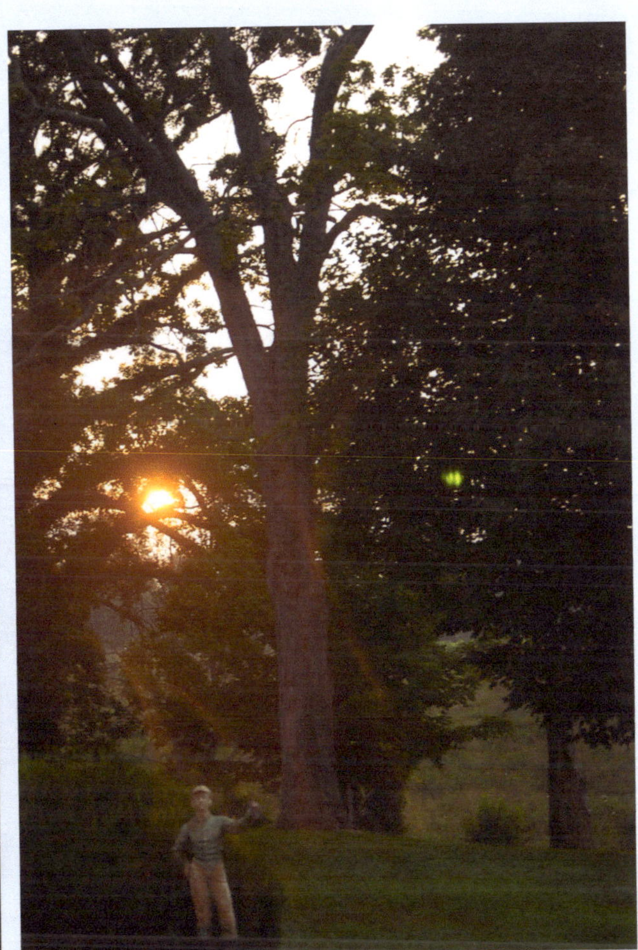

You are the light of the world.
A town built on a hill cannot be hidden.
Neither do people light a lamp and put it under a bowl.
Instead they put it on its stand, and it gives light to everyone in the house.
MATTHEW 5:14-15 (NIV)

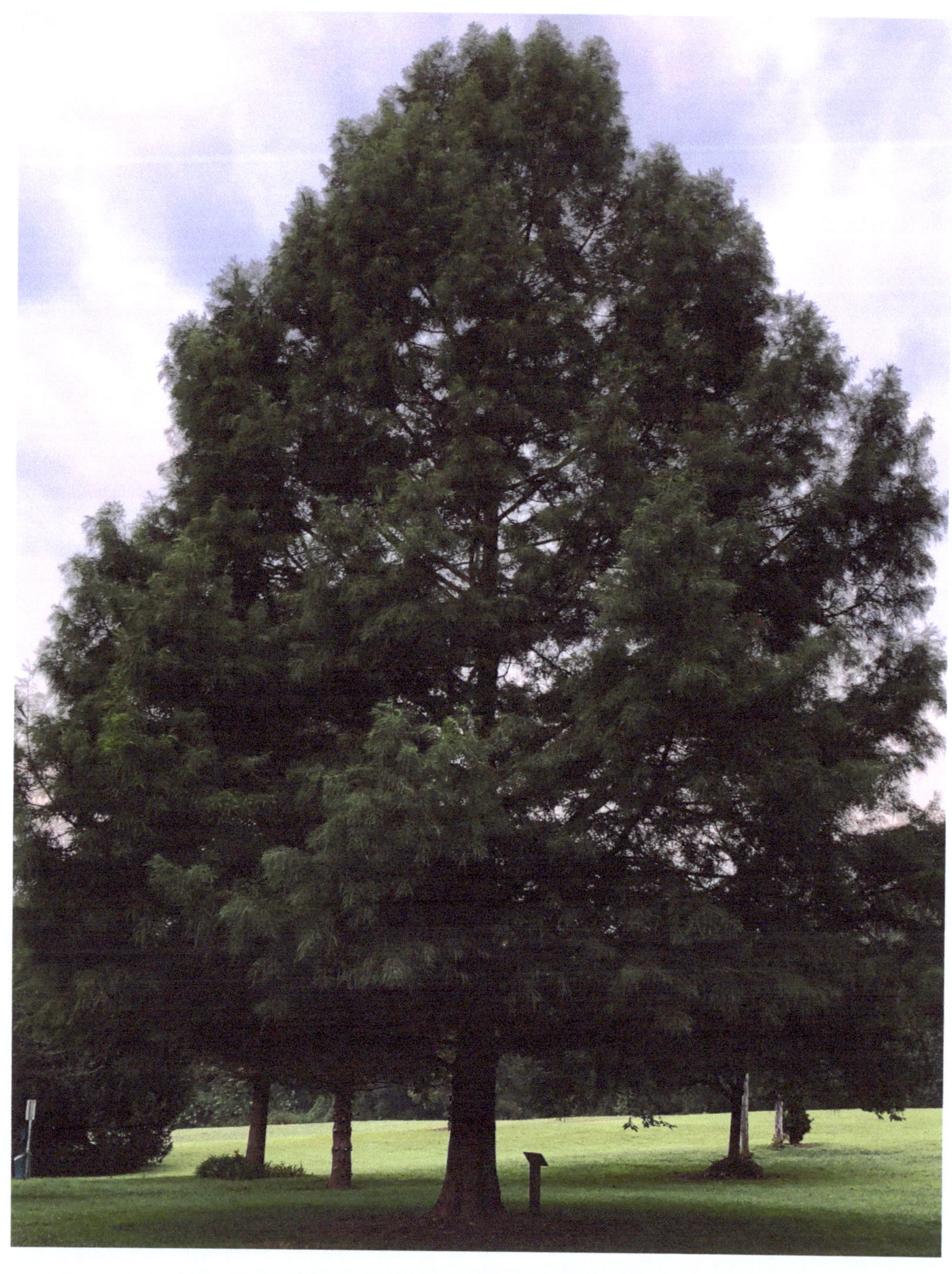

*Hope deferred
makes the heart sick,
But desire fulfilled
is a tree of life.*
PROVERBS 13:12 (NASB)

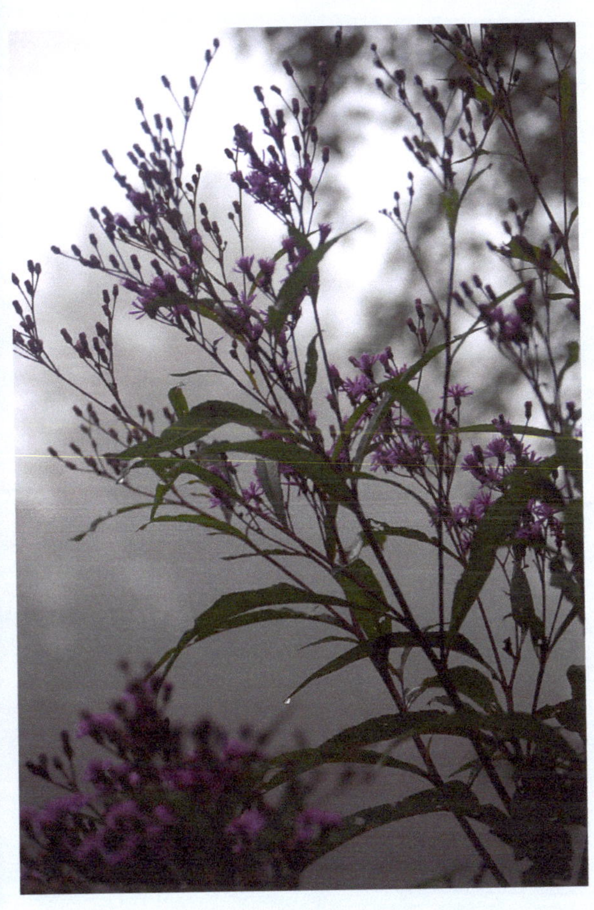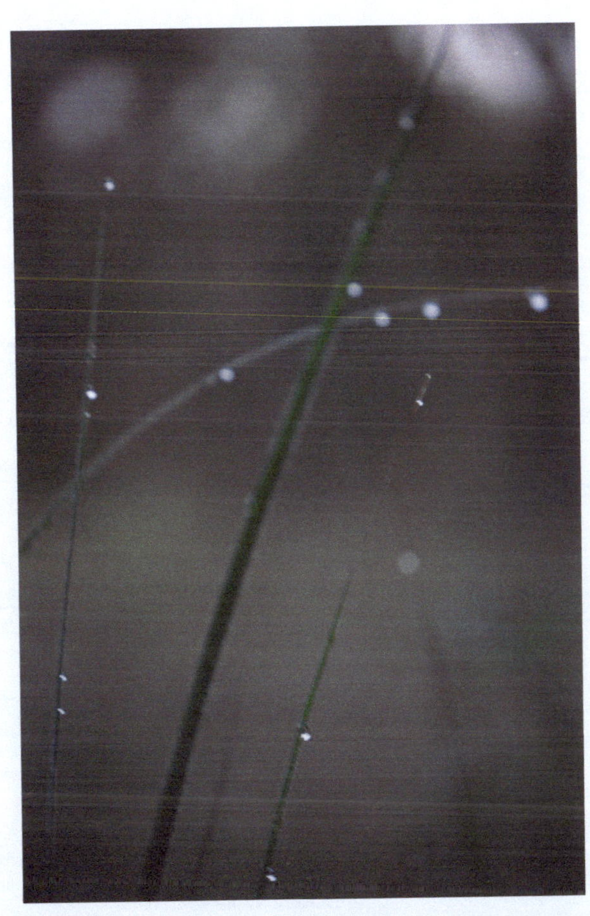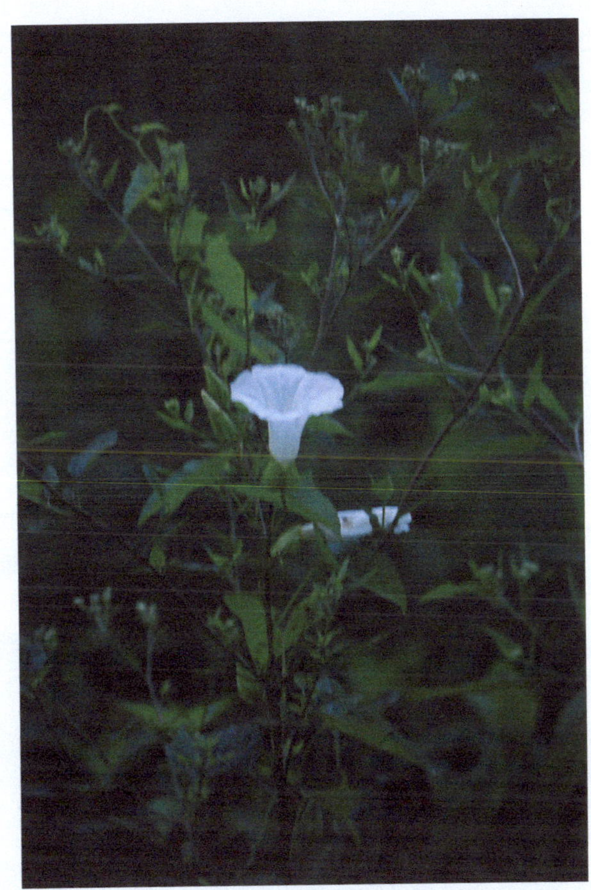

Weeping may last for the night,
But a shout of joy comes in the morning.
PSALM 30:5 (NASB)

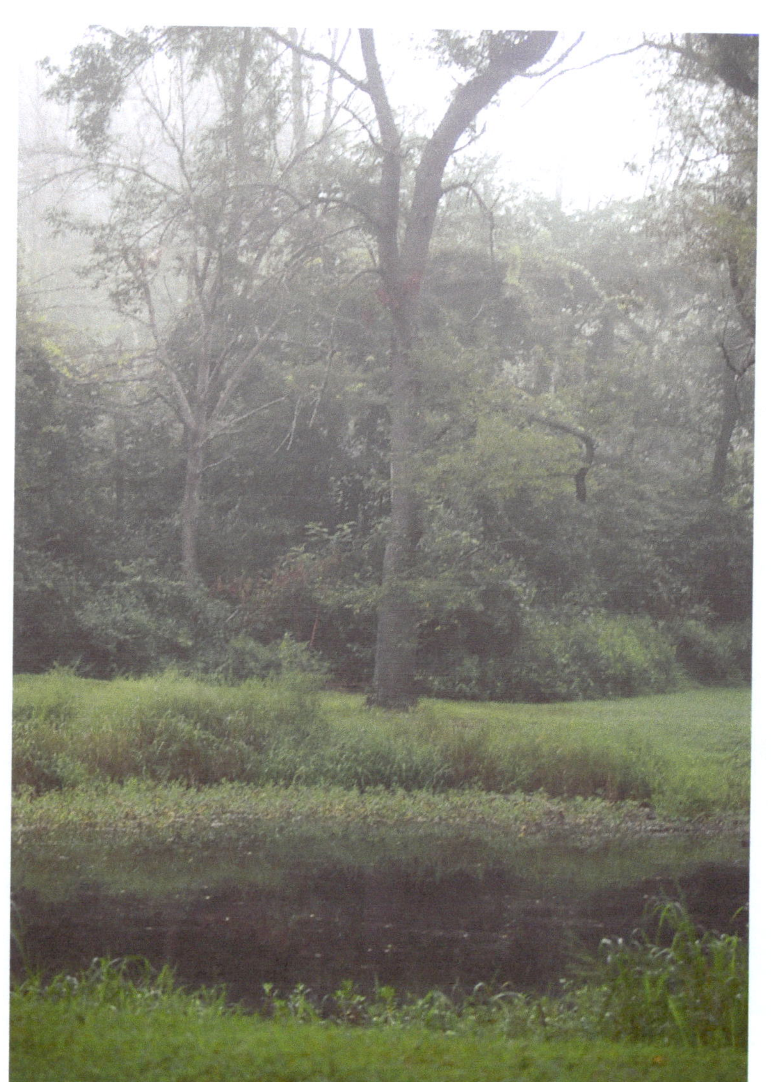
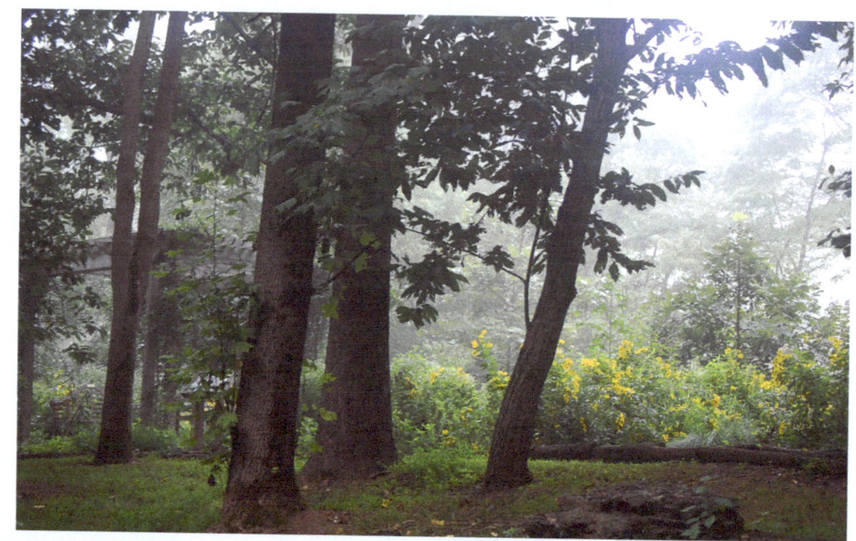
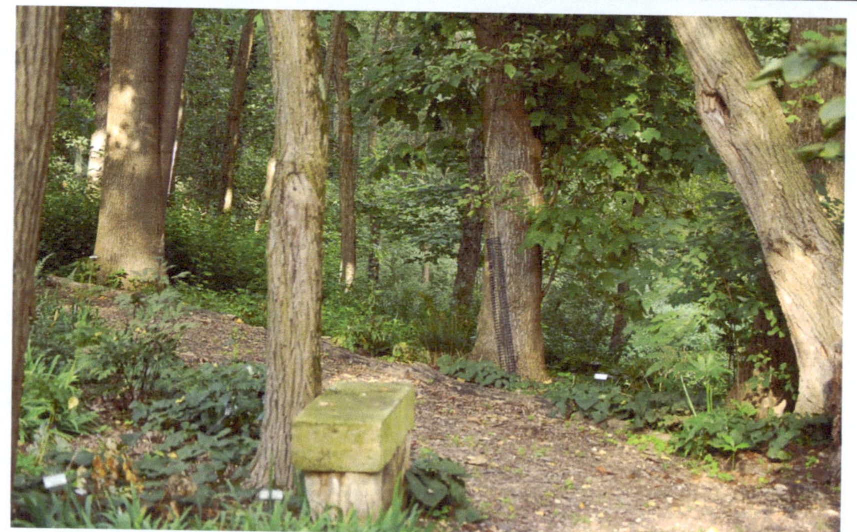

Answer me when I call to you, my righteous God.
Give me relief from my distress;
have mercy on me and hear my prayer.
PSALM 4:1 (NIV)

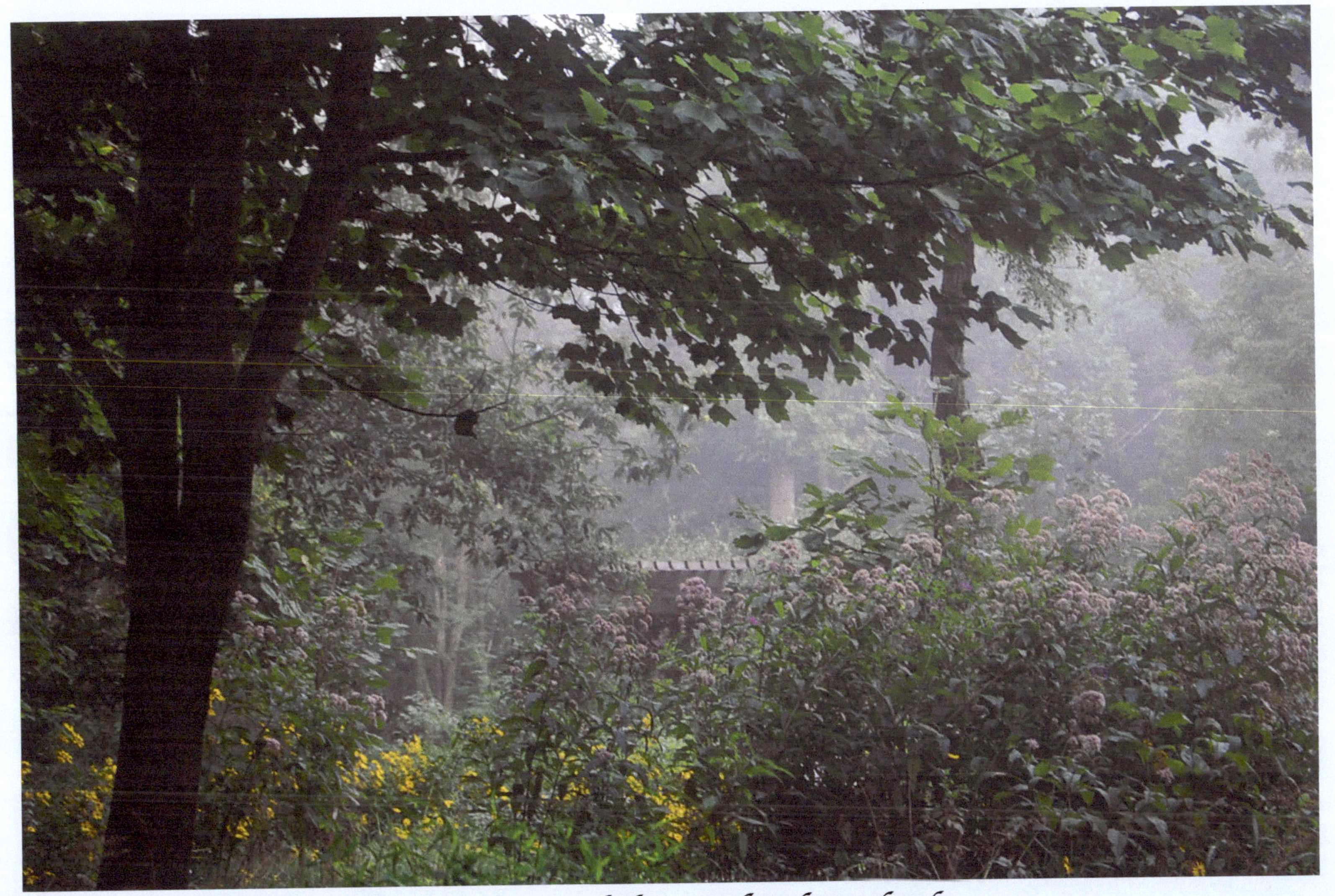

For as the earth brings forth its bud,
As the garden causes things that are sown in it to spring forth,
So the LORD GOD will cause righteousness and praise
to spring forth before all nations.
ISAIAH 61:11 (NKJV)

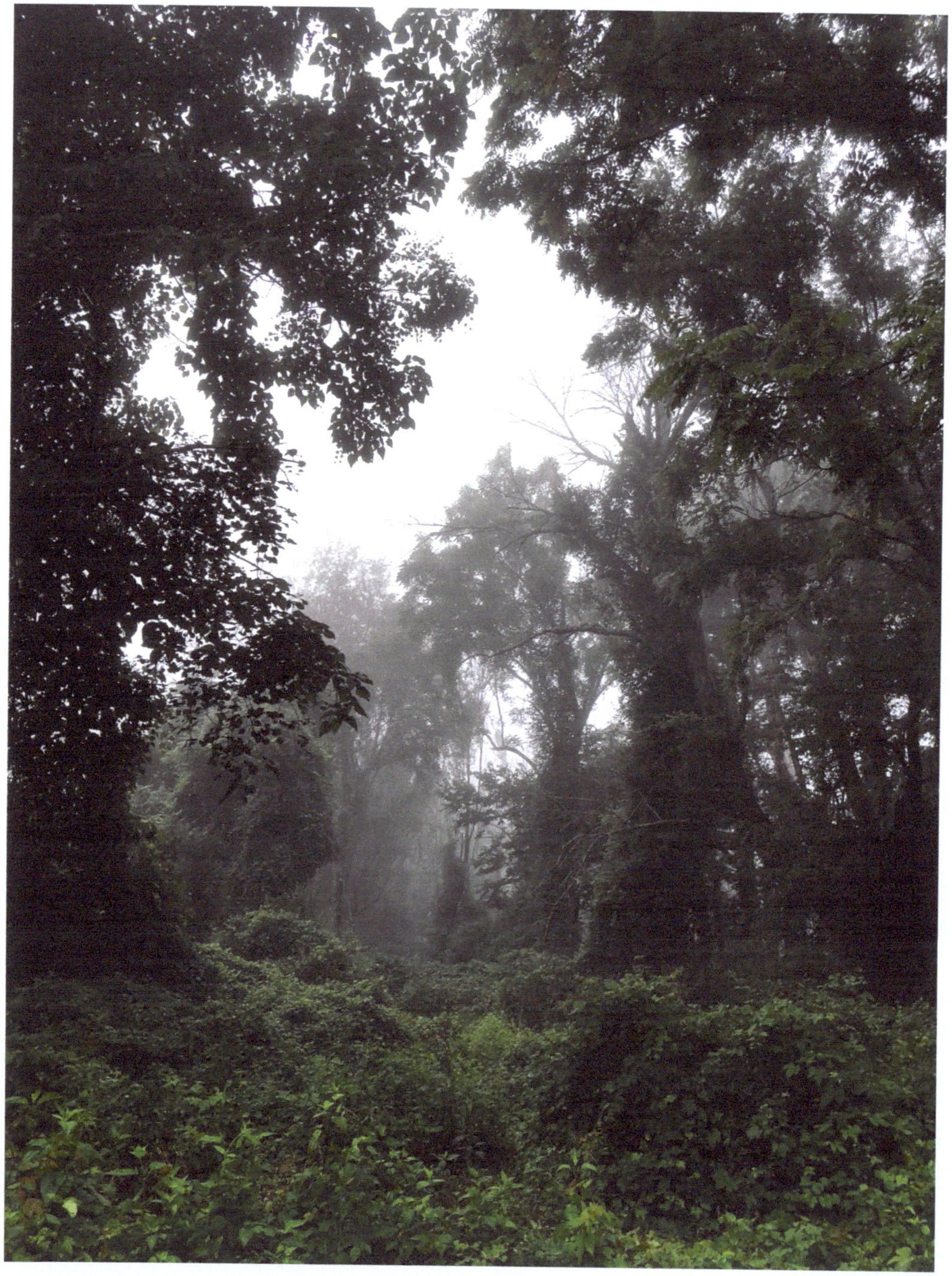

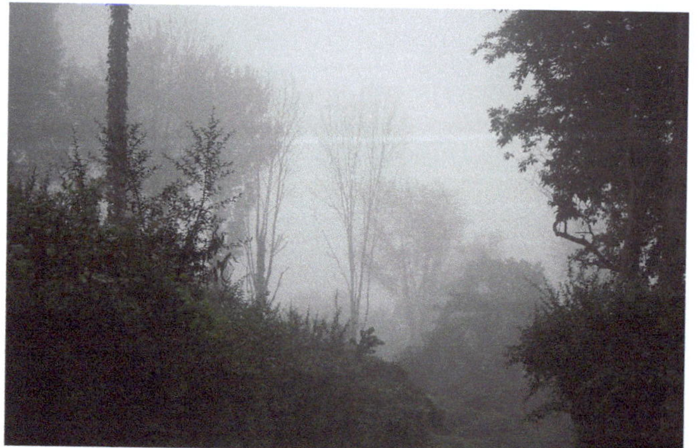

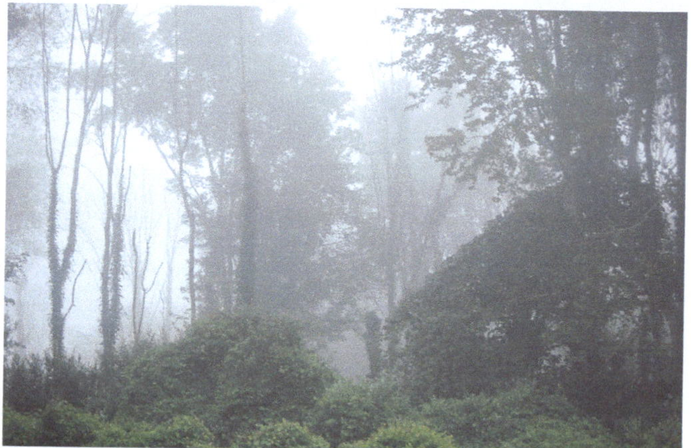

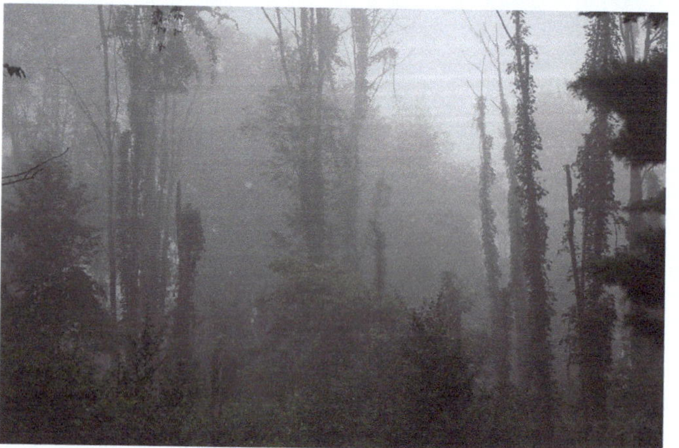

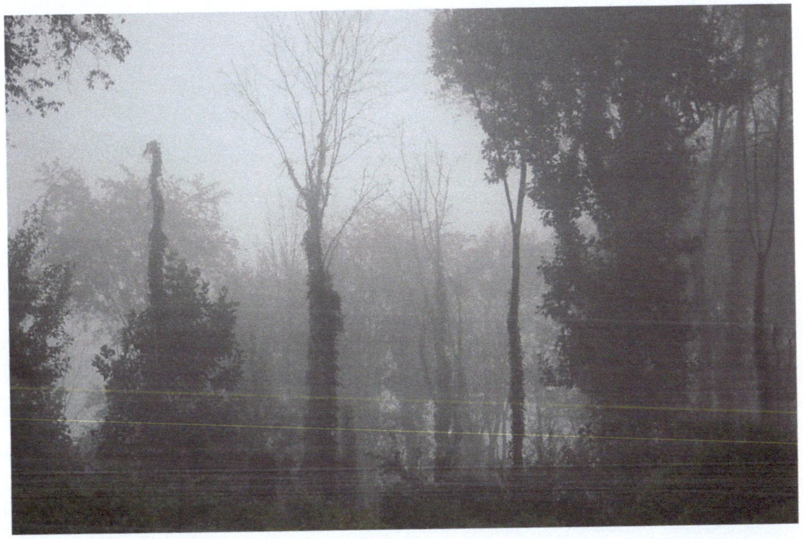

'Do not fear, for I am with you;
Do not anxiously look about you,
for I am your God.
I will strengthen you, surely I will help you,
Surely I will uphold you
with My righteous right hand.'
ISAIAH 41:10 (NASB)

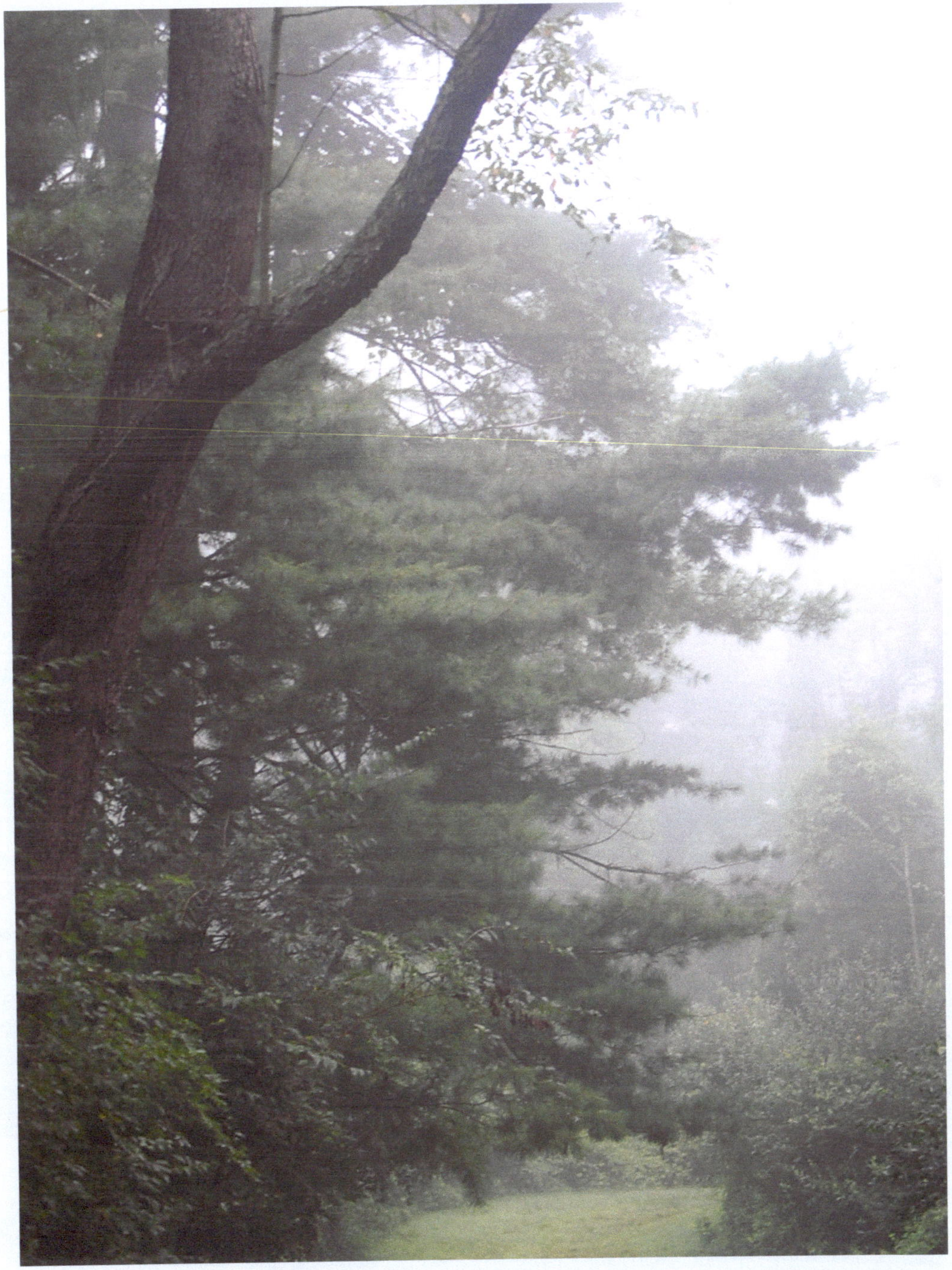

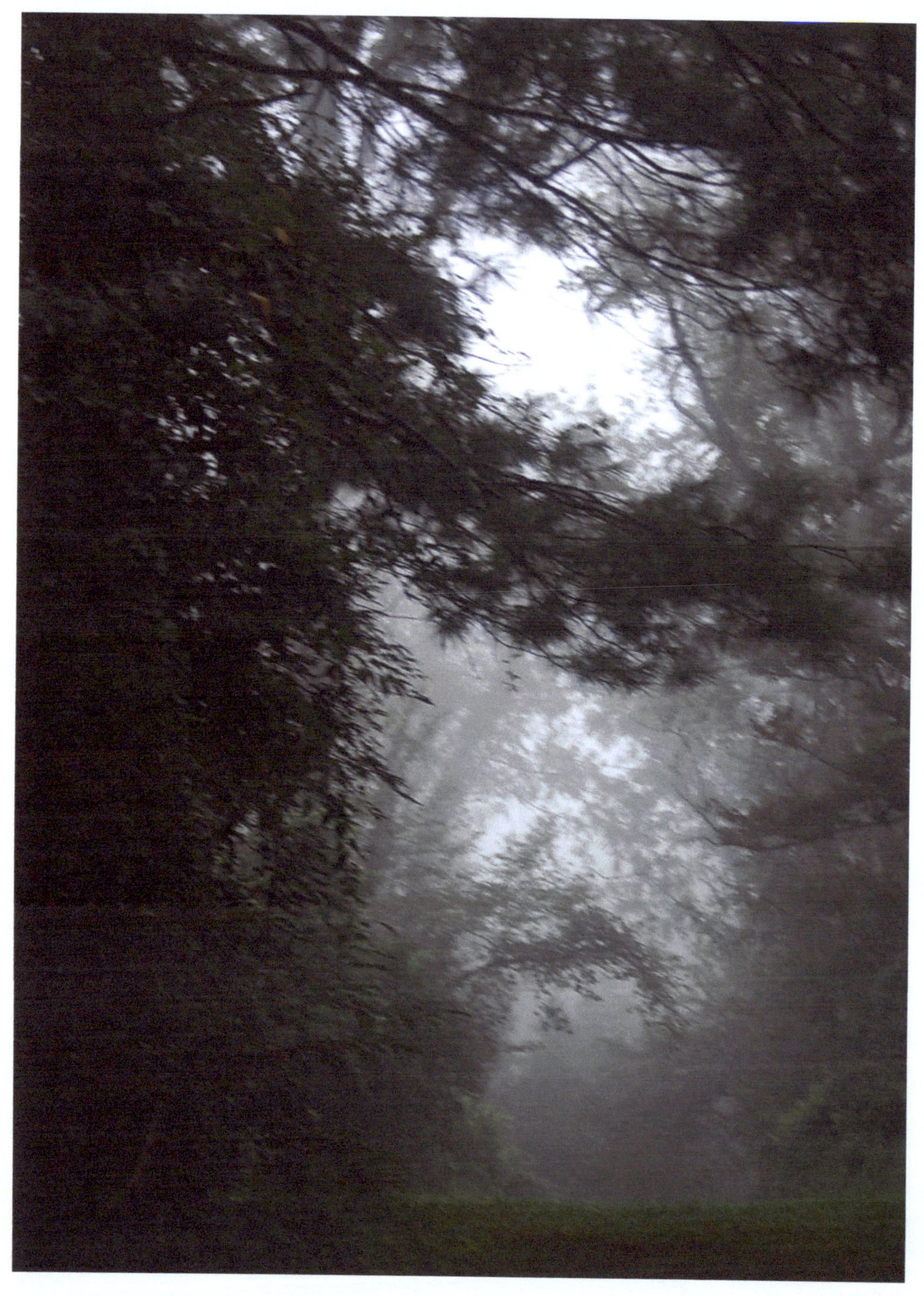

We don't yet see things clearly.
We're squinting in a fog,
peering through a mist.
But it won't be long before the
weather clears and the sun shines bright!
We'll see it all then,
see it all as clearly as God sees us,
knowing him directly just as he knows us!
1 CORINTHIANS 13:12 (MSG)

And I will lead the blind
in a way that they do not know,
in paths that they have not known
I will guide them.
I will turn the darkness before them into light,
the rough places into level ground.
These are the things I do,
and I do not forsake them.
ISAIAH 42:16 (ESV)

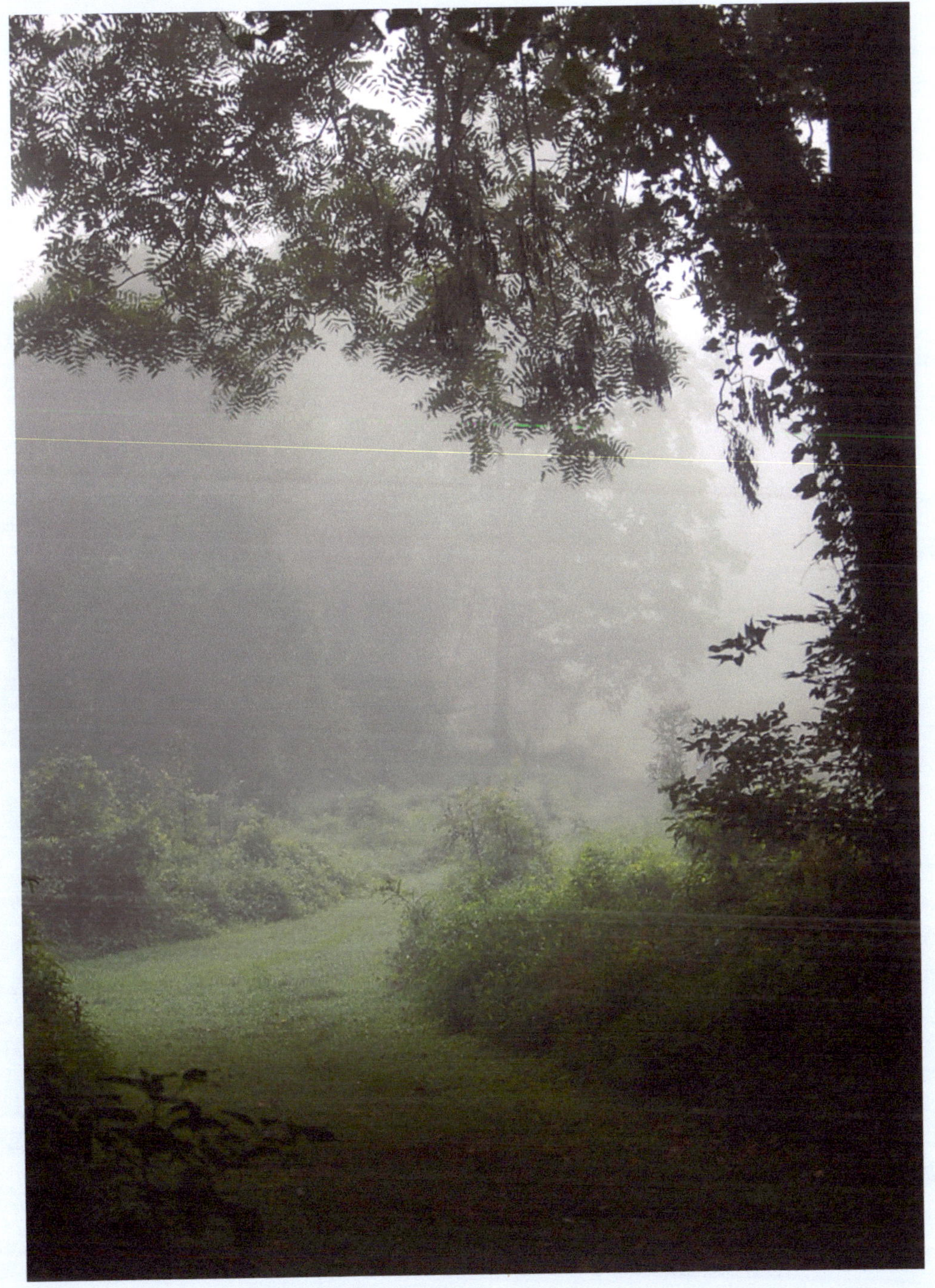

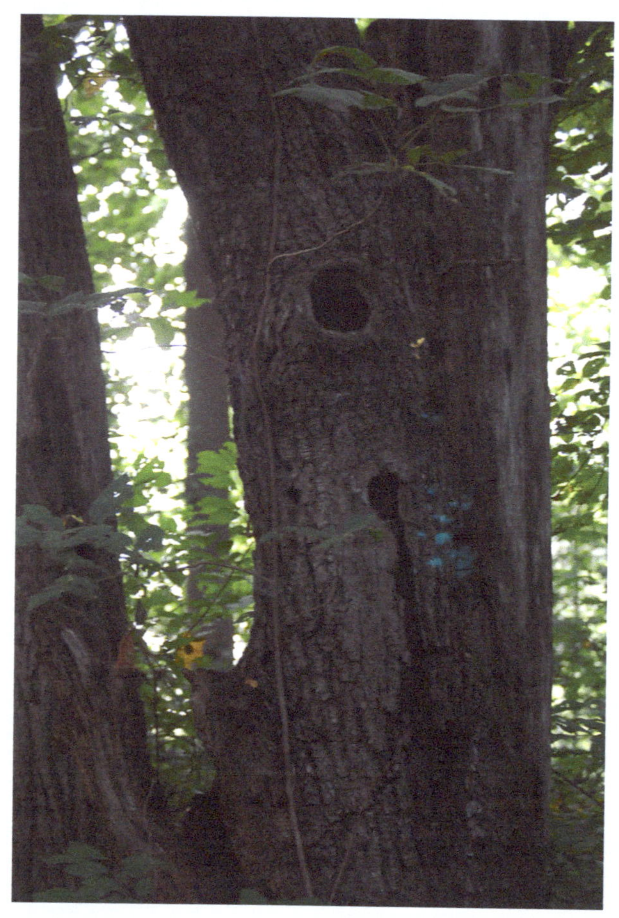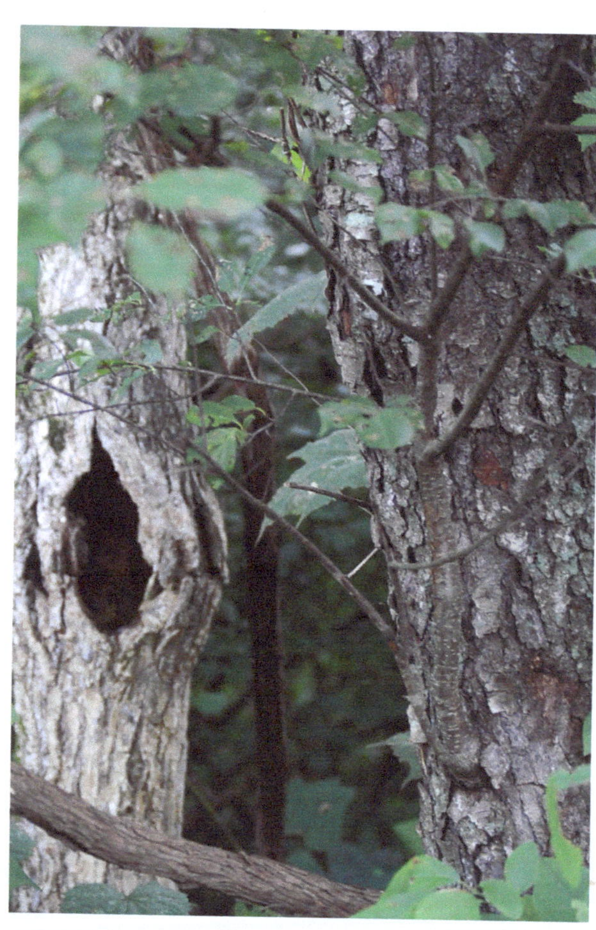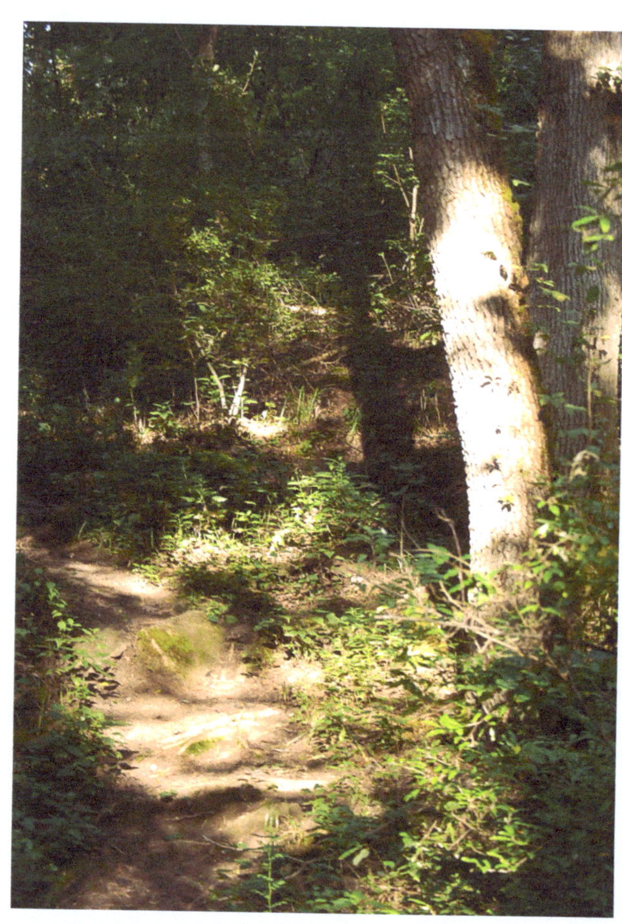

You are a hiding place for me;
You preserve me from trouble;
You surround me with shouts of deliverance. Selah
PSALM 32:7 (NKJV)

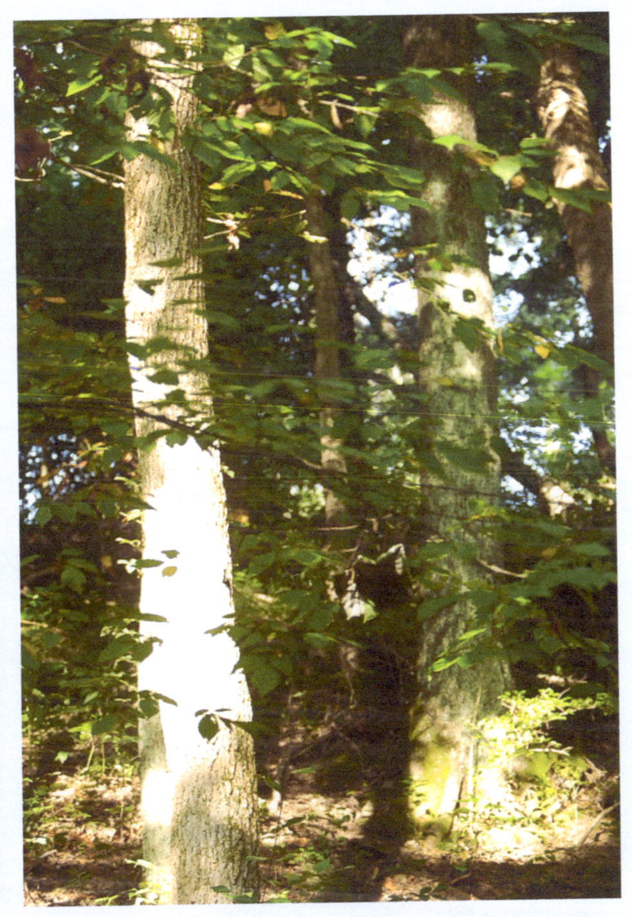
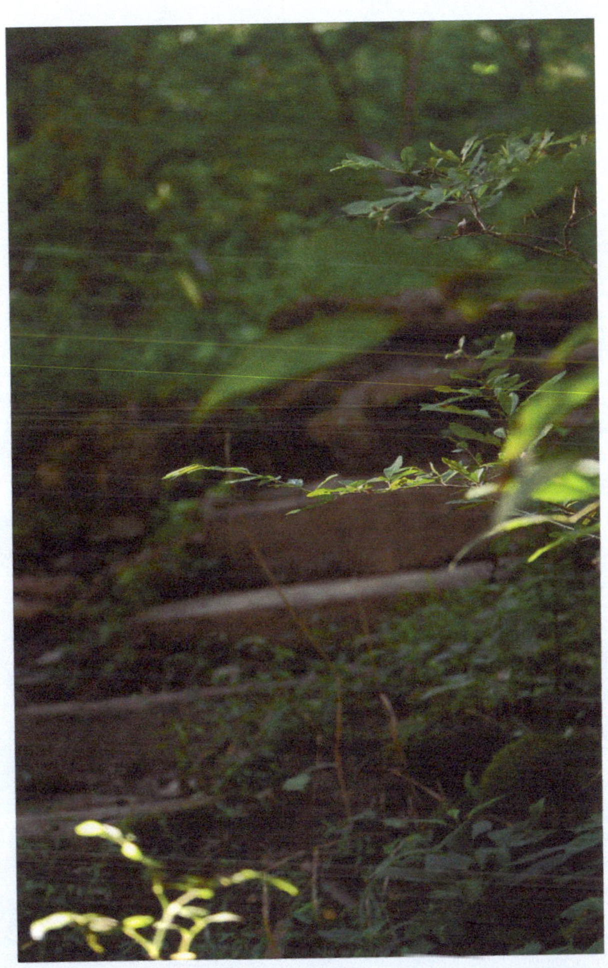
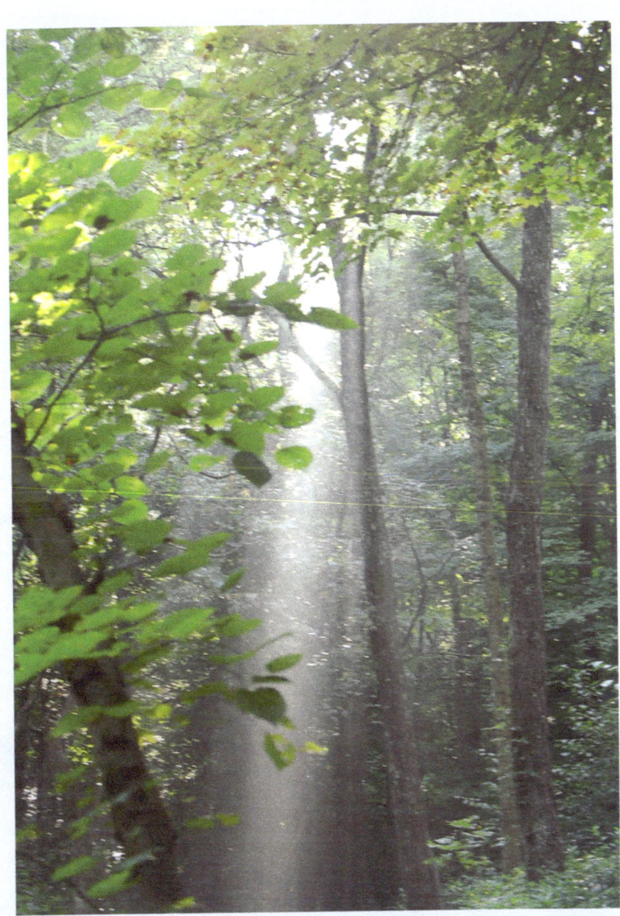

But the plans of the LORD stand firm forever,
the purposes of his heart through all generations.
PSALM 33:11 (NIV)

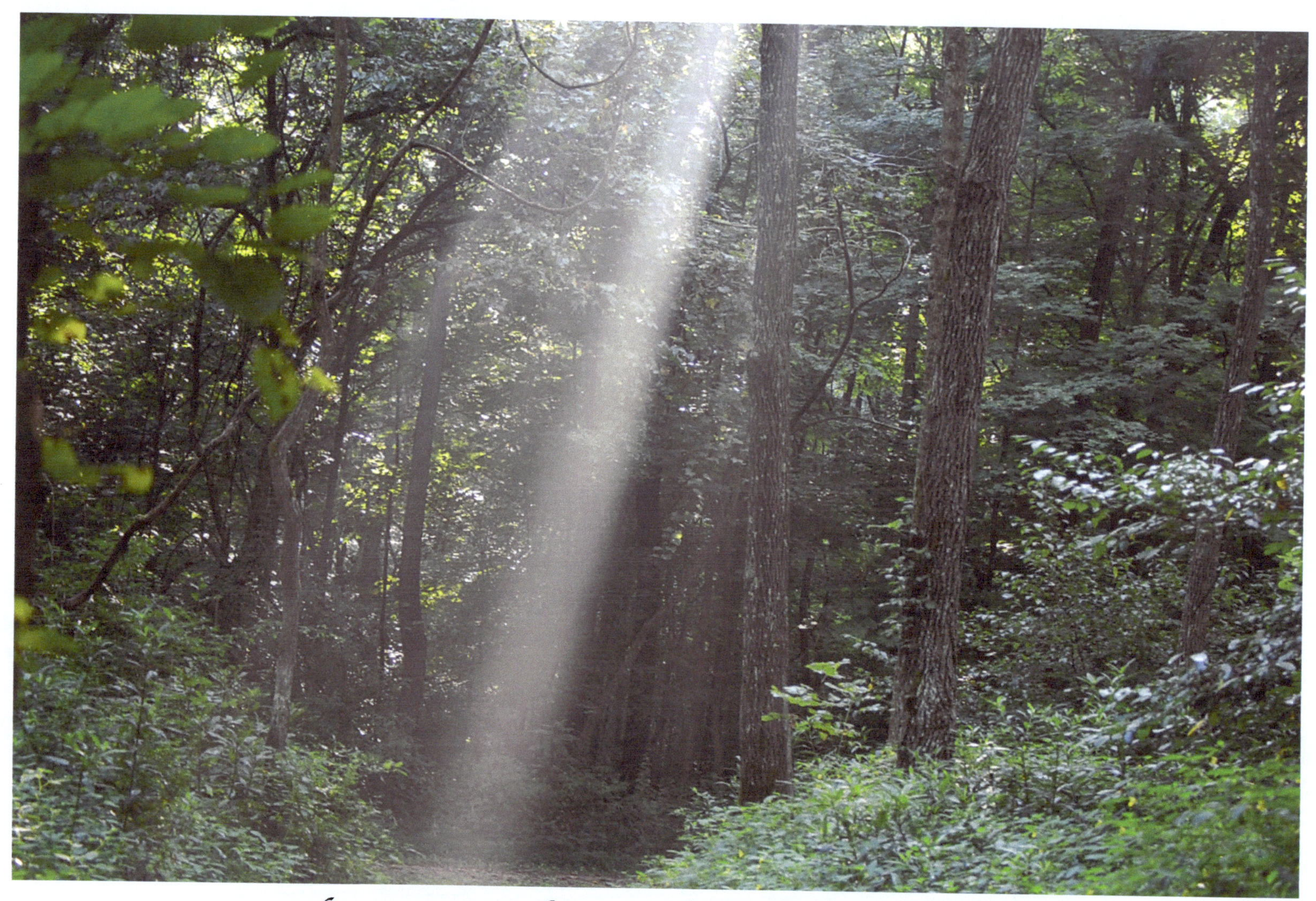

In the same way, let your light shine before others,
that they may see your good deeds
and glorify your Father in heaven.
MATTHEW 5:16 (NIV)

"I am the LORD;
I have called you in righteousness;
I will take you by the hand and keep you;
I will give you a covenant for the people,
a light for the nations,
to open the eyes that are blind..."
ISAIAH 42:6-7 (ESV)

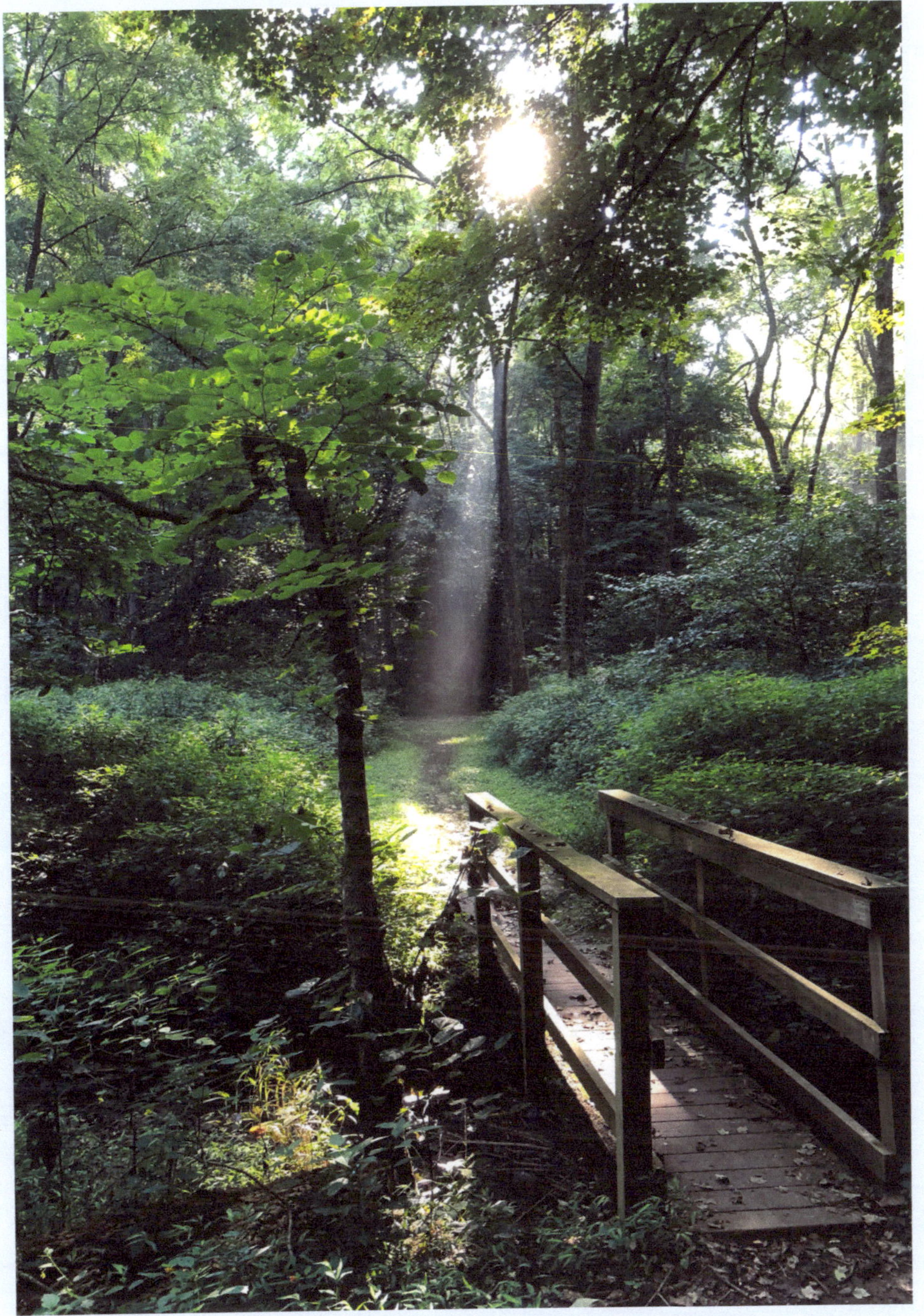

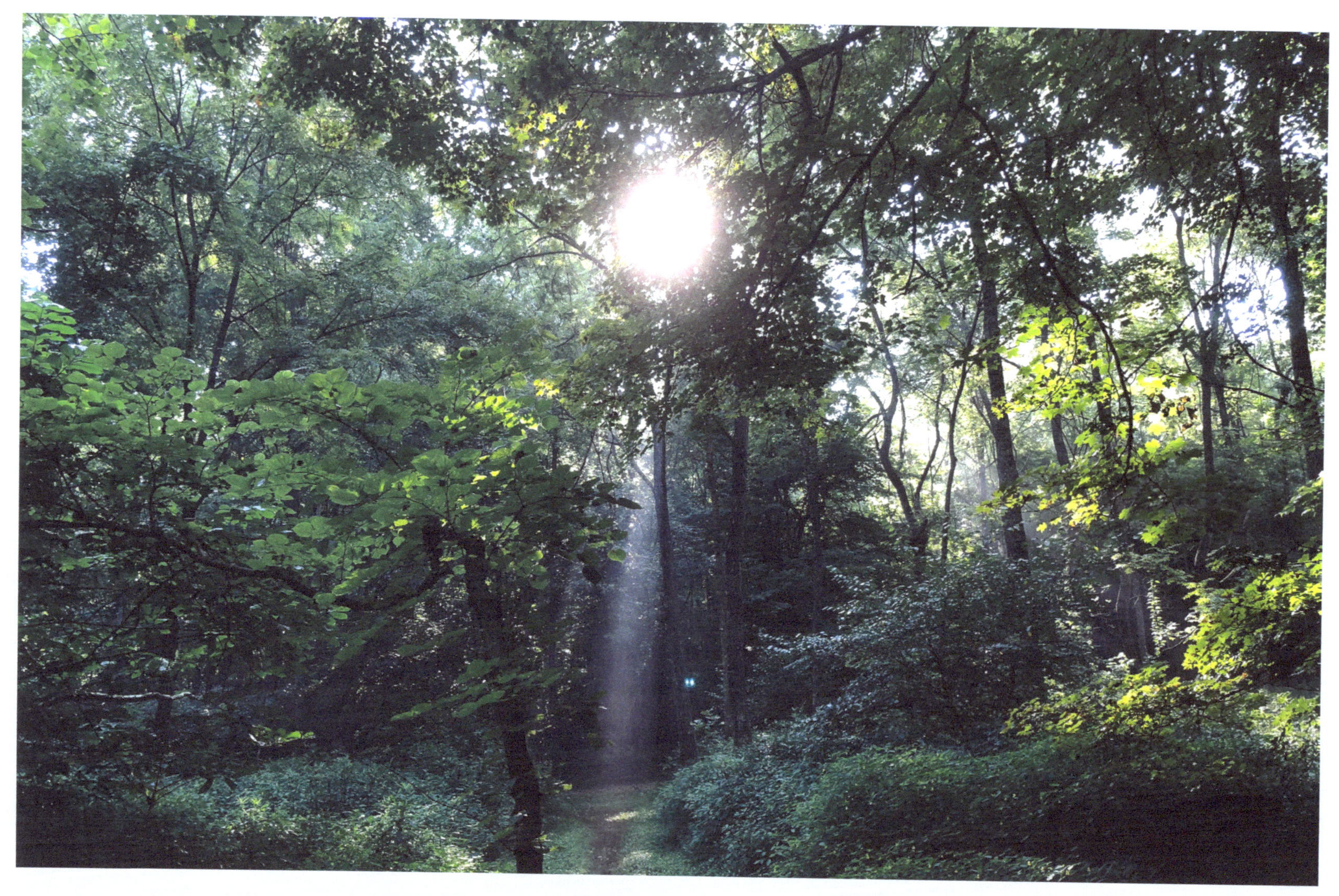

'May the LORD bless you and protect you.
May the LORD smile on you and be gracious to you.
May the LORD show you his favor and give you his peace.'
NUMBERS 6:25-26 (NLT)

ABOUT THE ACREE'S

Karin is a hard-working wife and mother of two lovely teenage daughters. Daily work and family demands are juggled with agile imperfection. To remain centered, and as time permits, she likes to cook, work out at the Y, play piano, paint (her husband Tony claims she's addicted), read, and to commune with nature--and with God--hiking through the woods.

ACKNOWLEDGEMENTS

I mindfully and prayerfully compiled this scripture photo book of numerous treks through the Creasey Mahan Nature Preserve with the guidance of many family and friends. I am grateful, and blessed, by your unwavering love and support for me and my family. And my heartfelt thanks, also, to Tavia Brown and the entire staff at Creasey Mahan Nature Preserve, for your passion and dedication to conservation and transforming the Preserve into a serene outdoor sanctuary for us all to play in and enjoy.

ABOUT THE CREASEY MAHAN NATURE PRESERVE

Creasey Mahan Nature Preserve is located at 12501 Harmony Landing Road located in beautiful Goshen, Kentucky, which is approximately 30 minutes east of Louisville, Kentucky and 20 minutes west of La Grange, Kentucky. Creasey Mahan Nature Preserve is a non-profit public charity established in 1975 through the legacy of Virginia Creasey Mahan and Howard Mahan. The Nature Preserve is a 170-acre family friendly destination in Goshen that offers a complete family experience. In 2017 alone, 48,000 visitors were served through monthly events, school field trips, athletic practices and races, fun programs, and community gatherings.

The Preserve maintains three historic buildings and offers a natural history museum for educational programs. With over 9 miles of wooded trails that weave through open grasslands and four year-round springs and waterfalls, Creasey Mahan Nature Preserve is a wonderful place to relax and take a leisurely hike. Families may enjoy using Harmony Park playground, and visit the library in the Preserve's old dairy and tobacco barn. They may also have a picnic, camp overnight, walk their dog(s), and fly a kite in one of the open grassy areas. Creasey Mahan Nature Preserve offers something for everyone!

For more information, please visit:
http://www.creaseymahannaturepreserve.org

Creasey Mahan Nature Preserve
12501 Harmony Landing Road
Goshen, Kentucky 40026
Phone: 502-228-4362
General email: Info@KYNaturepreserve.org

CREASEY MAHAN NATURE PRESERVE MAP

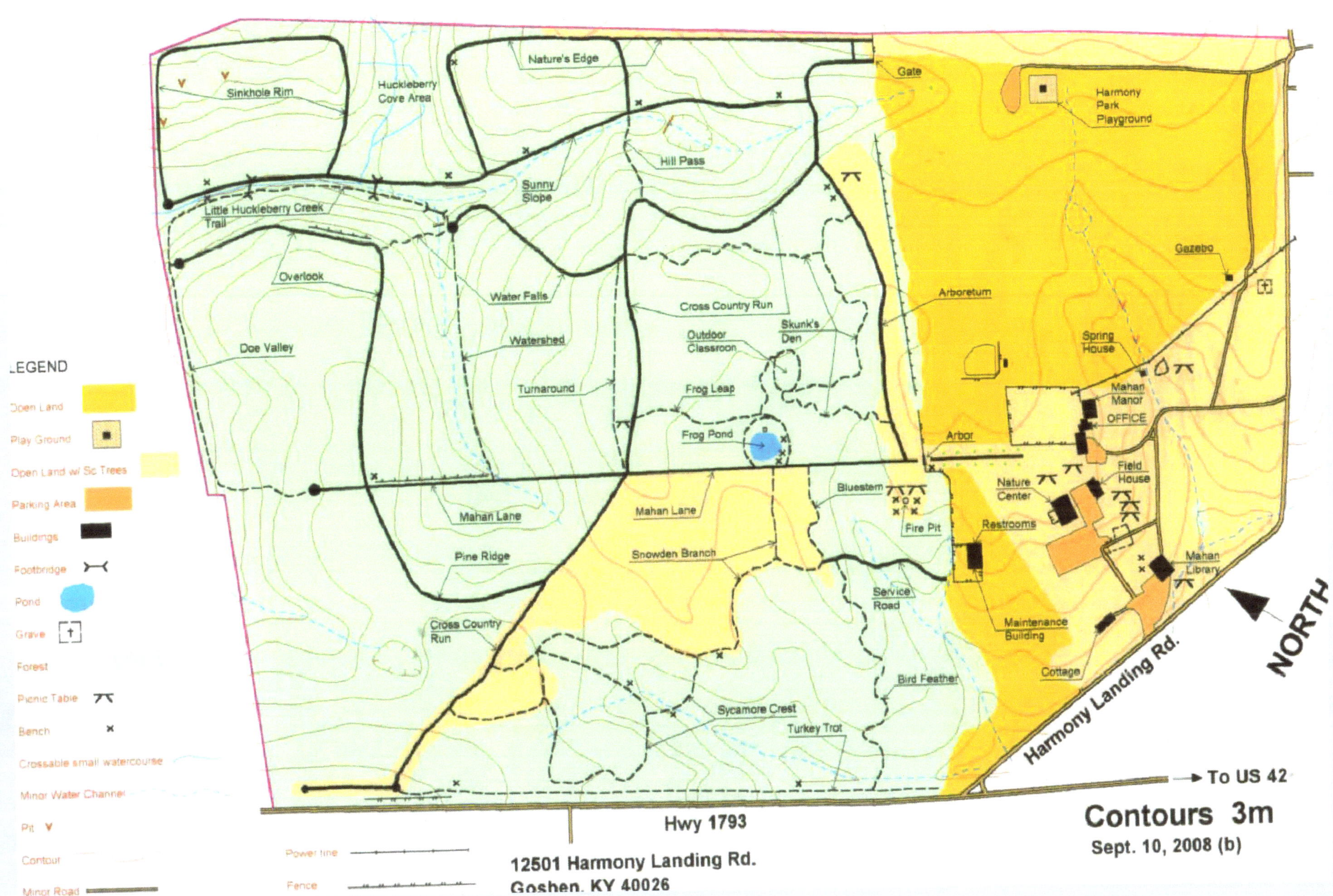